D0374207

VELOCITIES

Books by Stephen Dobyns

POETRY

Velocities: New and Selected Poems, 1966–1992 (1994)
Body Traffic (1990)
Cemetery Nights (1987)
Black Dog, Red Dog (1984)
The Balthus Poems (1982)
Heat Death (1980)
Griffon (1976)
Concurring Beasts (1971)

NOVELS

The Wrestler's Cruel Study (1993)
Saratoga Haunting (1993)
After Shocks/Near Escapes (1991)
Saratoga Hexameter (1990)
The House on Alexandrine (1990)
Saratoga Bestiary (1988)
The Two Deaths of Señora Puccini (1988)
A Boat Off the Coast (1987)
Saratoga Snapper (1986)
Cold Dog Soup (1985)
Saratoga Headhunter (1985)
Dancer with One Leg (1983)
Saratoga Swimmer (1981)
Saratoga Longshot (1976)
A Man of Little Evils (1973)

VELOCITIES

NEW AND SELECTED POEMS
1966–1992

STEPHEN DOBYNS

VIKING
PENGUIN BOOKS

VIKING
PENGUIN BOOKS
Published by the Penguin Group
Penguin Books USA Inc., 375 Hudson Street,
New York, New York 10014, U.S.A.
Penguin Books Ltd, 27 Wrights Lane,
London W8 5TZ, England
Penguin Books Australia Ltd, Ringwood,
Victoria, Australia
Penguin Books Canada Ltd, 10 Alcorn Avenue,
Toronto, Ontario, Canada M4V 3B2
Penguin Books (N.Z.) Ltd, 182–190 Wairau Road,
Auckland 10, New Zealand

Penguin Books Ltd, Registered Offices:
Harmondsworth, Middlesex, England

First published in 1994 in simultaneous hardcover and paperback editions by
Viking Penguin and Penguin Books, divisions of Penguin Books USA Inc.

10 9 8 7 6 5 4 3 2 1

Copyright © Stephen Dobyns, 1994
All rights reserved

Pages ix–xi constitute an extension of this copyright page.

LIBRARY OF CONGRESS CATALOGING IN PUBLICATION DATA
Dobyns, Stephen, 1941–
Velocities : new and selected poems, 1966–1992 / Stephen Dobyns.
p.   cm.
ISBN 0-670-83089-5 (hardcover)
ISBN 0 14 058.651 2 (paperback)
I. Title.
PS3554.02V45   1994
811'.54—dc20   93-17969

Printed in the United States of America
Set in Bembo
Designed by Claire Naylon Vaccaro

Without limiting the rights under copyright reserved above, no part of this
publication may be reproduced, stored in or introduced into a retrieval system,
or transmitted, in any form or by any means (electronic, mechanical, photocopying,
recording or otherwise), without the prior written permission of both the
copyright owner and the above publisher of this book.

For Isabel

ACKNOWLEDGMENTS

Acknowledgments are due to the editors of the following publications in whose pages the new poems in this book first appeared:

Borderlands: "Santiago: Five Men in the Street: Number One," "Santiago: La Avenida Pedro de Valdivia," "Santiago: Market Day in Winter."
Gettysburg Review: "Red Geraniums," "Roughhousing."
Harvard Review: "Santiago: Five Men in the Sreet: Number Two."
The Paris Review: "Fatal Kisses," "Favorite Iraqi Soldier."
Phoebe: "Santiago: In Praise of Community," "Uprising."
Ploughshares: "The Community," "Pastel Dresses," "Santiago: Forestal Park," "Somewhere It Still Moves," "Tenderly."
Salmagundi: "Hidden Within the Sleeves of Those Dark Robes," "Syracuse Nights," "Topless."

"Favorite Iraqi Soldier" also appeared in *The Best Poems 1992*, edited by Louise Gluck, published in 1993 by Charles Scribner's Sons.

The author would like to thank Hayden Carruth, Louise Gluck, Joe-Anne McLaughlin-Carruth, and Ellen Bryant Voight for their invaluable help in the selection of the poems.

Concurring Beasts
Copyright © Stephen Dobyns, 1971
Originally published by Atheneum

"Passing the Word," "Contingencies," "Counterparts," "Name-burning," and "The Ways of Keys" first appeared in *Poetry*; "Leaving the Bar and Low Life at Closing, I Unsuccessfully Pursue Sainthood," "Connections," and "Refusing the Necessary" in *Kayak*; "In the Hospital" in *Poetry Northwest*; "After the War with the Eskimos" and "Explaining the Nature of Evidence" (as "Straight but Not Blue") in *The Chicago Review*; "The Conviviality of Cows" in *Cafe Solo*; and "The Way It Goes or the Proper Use of Leisure Time" in *The North American Review*.

Griffon
Copyright © Stephen Dobyns, 1976
Originally published by Atheneum

"Six Poems on Moving" and "Clouds" first appeared in *Poetry*; "Putting It All Away" in *New Letters*; "The Men with Long Faces" in *Seneca Review*; "The Grandfather Poem," "Envy," "Spite," "Grief," and "Silence" in *The New Yorker*; "Cross-roads," "Covetousness," and "Absence" in *Bird Effort*; "Seeing Off a Friend" in *Antaeus*; "Sloth" and "Gluttony" in *Kayak*; and "Anger" and "Bravado" in *Pequod*.

Heat Death
Copyright © Stephen Dobyns, 1980
Originally published by Atheneum

"Rain Song" and "The Delicate, Plummeting Bodies" first appeared in *The New Yorker*; "Oatmeal Deluxe," "A Separate Time," "Morning Song," "Song for Making the Birds Come," "It's Like This," and "A Place in Maine" in *Poetry*; "Song of the Drowned Boy" and "Song of Four Dancers" in *Kayak*; "The Body of Romulus" in *Ironwood*; "Fear" in *The Virginia Quarterly Review*; "Letter Beginning with the First Line of Your Letter" and "Footstep" in *Pequod*; "Fragments" and "Song of the Wrong Response" in *The Iowa Review*; "Geese" in *The Missouri Review*; "Separations" in *Ploughshares*; and "Pablo Neruda" in *The North American Review*.

The Balthus Poems
Copyright © Stephen Dobyns, 1982
Originally published by Atheneum

"The Greedy Child," "The Guitar Lesson," "The Room," "The Mountain," "The Triangular Field," "Katia Reading," and "The Street" first appeared in *Poetry*; "The Card Game" in *Kayak*; "Getting Up" and "The Window" in *The New Yorker*; "The Room" and "Gottéron Landscape" in *The Black Warrior Review*; "The White Skirt" in *Antaeus*; and "Japanese Girl with Red Table" in *The North American Review*.

Black Dog, Red Dog
Copyright © Stephen Dobyns, 1984
Originally published by Holt, Rinehart and Winston

"The Gun" first appeared in *Antaeus*; "Birth Report," "Under the Green Ceiling," "Wind Chimes," "This Life," "Black Dog, Red Dog," "Frenchie," "The Great Doubters of History," "Night Swimmer," and "Dead Baby" in *The American Poetry Review*; "General Matthei Drives Home Through Santiago" in *Poetry*; "Dancing in Vacationland" in *The Black Warrior Review*; "Bleeder" and "Kentucky Derby Day, Belfast, Maine" in *Kayak*; "Where We Are" in *Blue Fish*; "Cuidadores de Autos" and "What You Have Come to Expect" in *The New Yorker*; and "Beauty" in *Crazyhorse*.

Cemetery Nights
Copyright © Stephen Dobyns, 1987
Published by Viking Penguin

"The Gardener" and "The General and the Tango Singer" first appeared in *The Virginia Quarterly Review*; "Tomatoes," "Marsyas, Midas and the Barber," "White Pig," "To Pull Into Oneself as Into a Locked Room," and "The Nihilist" in *The American Poetry Review*; "How to Like It" in *Ploughshares*; "Waking" and "Streetlight" in *Pequod*; "Faces" in *Quarterly West*; "Cemetery Nights II" in *The New England Review*; "Spiritual Chickens" and "Cemetery Nights IV" in *Seneca Review*; "Bowlers Anonymous" in *Raccoon*; "Theseus Within the Labyrinth," "Querencia," and "Cemetery Nights V" in *Poetry*; and "Mermaid" and "The Noise the Hairless Make" in *Sonora Review*.

"Cemetery Nights" appeared in *Singular Voices: American Poetry Today*, edited by Stephen Berg (Avon, 1985), and in *New American Poets of the 80's*, edited by Jack Myers and Roger Weingarten (Wampeter Press, 1985). "How to Like It" later appeared in *The Bread Loaf Anthology of Contemporary American Poetry*, edited by Robert Pack, Sydney Lea, and Jay Parini (University Press of New England, 1985).

Body Traffic
Copyright © Stephen Dobyns, 1990
Published by Viking Penguin

"The Body's Journey" and "Spleen" first appeared in *The Virginia Quarterly Review*; "The Belly," "Careers," "Receivers of the World's Attention," and "The Body's Weight" in *The American Poetry Review*; "Desire," "The Body's Curse," and "The Body's Hope" in *Antaeus*; "Rootless," "Long Story," and "Freight Cars" in *Poetry*; "Eyelids," "Sweat," "The Body's Strength," and "Slipping Away" in *The Paris Review*; "No Map" and "How Could You Ever Be Fine" in *Ironweed*; "Confession" and "The Day the World Ends" in *Ploughshares*; "In a Row" in *Onthebus*; "Shaving" in *Special Report: Fiction*; "The Music One Looks Back On" in *The Gettysburg Review*; "How It Was at the End" in *Indiana Review*; "Walls to Put Up, Walls to Take Down" in *CutBank*; and "Toting It Up" in *Boulevard*.

CONTENTS

FROM BLACK DOG, RED DOG (1984)

VELOCITIES

NEW POEMS

SANTIAGO: FIVE MEN IN THE STREET: NUMBER ONE

Four fellows in orange uniforms
and a fifth in a dismal suit play
pickup soccer in the street. It's their

lunch break, and the ball, a kid's beach ball,
might not make it through this half hour
of pleasure, as the men leap and kick

this flimsy target of blue plastic.
The guy in the suit is a clerk who
gets yelled at. The ones in orange sweep

out a garage for a boss who thinks
a uniform looks sharp. The hours
they travel by bus to get to work,

the pennies they get paid, the verbal
abuse of those who need to prove they're
cut from better cloth—all disappear

in this thirty minutes in the street.
It's the end of winter and the tightly
folded leaves of the plane trees begin

to release their delicate green plumes.
The clerk lunges for a kick that shoots
the ball smack against a metal gate.

Goal! shout the others. The clerk raises
his hands above his head as his pals
whack him on the back. Take this moment

and freeze it—five guys grinning, showing off
their lousy teeth. Not one will ever
find an easy death and each will know

a hundred forms of grief. Having gone
splat, the ball deflates on the pavement.
The five men collapse beneath a tree

and the clerk hands round his cigarettes.
They light up, sigh, and watch the leaves
unfurl their little flags of green.

SANTIAGO: FIVE MEN IN THE STREET: NUMBER TWO

In the back of a garbage truck parked on a side street,
five garbage collectors gobble a chocolate cake,
the gift of a lady each would like to squeeze a lot.

Sprawled in the gutter a black dog licks his dick
like there is no tomorrow, and no tomorrow either
for the five men eating with grubby fingers, smearing

the hand-cut slabs of thick black cake onto cheeks,
chins, noses and sometimes their mouths. That frosting
dribbles sweetness like a cut wrist drips blood

and they suck it from their fingernails and gulp down
the last crumbs. How disgusting! squawks a passing
matron to her friend. Had they fathomed the fullness

of the world's filth they would never have entrusted
their pristine garbage to these galoots. One puffs out
his cheeks to make a poot-poot noise like a fart,

and the matrons scuttle off to eat sweet creams and read
their lady poems. What a dreadful world! The immortal
verse of Keats versus a dog's red dick on the concrete.

Such contradictions make us rich. The black dog whacks
his tail against the sidewalk. These garbage guys
are his heroes and the dog reckons that if he's polite

all five will let him lick their fingers clean. The hot
sun baking his belly, his fleas idle for a change,
the prospect of sweet things in his mouth. Why, if he

could talk, he'd make a speech against the intellect,
art and math. What's so precious about what's not there?
Into the trash with Einstein and his furious sums!

Six blind women bustle along with arms linked
down the center of the sidewalk. One sells pencils,
another sings, a third peddles needles and pins.

Together they hurry as singly none would dare.
Who is in charge here? Faced with the accumulated
rush of all six, hooting at some private joke,

the merely sighted stumble from their path.
Oh, oh, here comes the big street! Red buses
vie to crush the unsighted and unsuspecting.

The women don't even know it's coming! Without
a pause in their exuberant dash, they burst
between two buses, which fan their sweaty cheeks,

and reach the other side (without suffering
a decrease in their audacity), then disappear.
But now come the sirens. How unfair! Have those

simple sightless souls been struck after all?
No, no, it was just an old poet whacked by a truck,
blinded by the excitement of completing his ode.

Brutal lips, slasher lips—as a stunned toddler
pecked by fifteen older female cousins carries the red
tokens of such oral stimulation so the elderly
bear the imprint of their endurance. Let's say

you hop off the porch and stomp on a nail. Ouch!
Well, that nail carves its caress, a thin crease
across the forehead. The summer day that Joey Dugan
wrecked your bike has left its mark. Your first orgasm,

those times you've guffawed and slapped your knee,
the time your canary died—each occasion imparts
a kiss, sometimes a single crease, sometimes a crease
upon a crease, sometimes a crease on top of that.

Consider the lateral slot which frustration chops
between the eyebrows. How many nasty moments have
gouged you there? Until it seems cavernous enough
for a coin, until death deposits its token and

trots you away. Cheeks, forehead, chin, baggy eyes,
even each earlobe displays a single traverse cut
until checking the mirror is like perusing the book
of your emotional life—all the laughter, all the tears.

That's not you, that's your diary—like a tablecloth
after a sumptuous meal, like bed sheets after a night
of making love—that's not you, that's scratch paper.
The real you, or so you claim, still throbs far beneath

all that jam, all that lipstick, all those tread marks.
Nowadays of course they can lift it off. Pay a fortune
to a plastic surgeon and snip snip he can pluck it
from your noggin just like you once stripped off

your football helmet. He'll set it on the table
where it will jiggle like a tub full of Jello.
What a life you've had! A face like a photo album,
a road map of good times. Its zigzagged lines resemble

evidence of erosion seen from the sky, the parched
red earth of some western town, a few cacti, a few
cattle on their last legs, and at this little joke,
your skull—all that's left of course—grins and grins.

FAVORITE IRAQI SOLDIER

Into his kit when sent to the front he had tucked
his black three-piece suit and through night
after night of the frightful bombing, which
not only wiped out but pragmatically entombed

his luckless comrades in a marvel of technological
decadence, he had kept the suit protected
so that at the surrender he had stripped naked
and slipped it on. This is when the photographer

caught him, that among the thousands of defeated
there walked one Iraqi in a three-piece suit
who tried to express by his general indifference
that he had stumbled into all this carnage simply

by accident and was now intent on strolling away.
I am a modest banker tossed on the wrong bus.
I am a humble stockbroker who took a wrong turn.
And he passed through the American lines

and began hitchhiking south. Did he elect
to relocate in Kuwait? Fat chance! Did he
want the lovable Saudis as new neighbors?
Quite unlikely! What about the opportunities

offered by the Libyans, Tunisians, Egyptians?
Truly hilarious! Was there any place in Africa
where he hoped to lay his head? Decidedly
not! What about Europe where he could start

as a servant or chop vegetables in the back
of a restaurant but work his way up? Completely
crazy! Or North America where he could dig
a ditch but with the right breaks might buy

a used car? Too ludicrous! What about South
America where he could pick fruit or Asia where
he could toil in a sweatshop? You must be nuts!
In his black suit he is already dressed for the part

and hopes to hitchhike to one of those Antarctic
islands and stroll around with the penguins.
Good evening Mr. White, good evening Mrs. Black,
your children swim quite nicely, they look

so hardy and fit. No one to give him orders
but the weather. No one to terrify him
but the occasional shark. No one to be mean to
but the little fish, who were put into this ocean

to serve him and whom he praises with each bite.
Thank you, gray brother, for the honor you have bestowed
on my belly. May you have the opportunity
to devour me when my days on earth are done.

It's not a fancy restaurant, nor is it
a dump and it's packed this Saturday night
when suddenly a man leaps onto his tabletop,
whips out his prick and begins sawing at it

with a butter knife. I can't stand it
anymore! he shouts. The waiters grab him
before he draws blood and hustle him
out the back. Soon the other diners return

to their fillets and slices of duck. How
peculiar, each, in some fashion, articulates.
Consider how the world implants a picture
in our brains. Maybe thirty people watched

this nut attack his member with a dull knife
and for each, forever after, the image pops up
a thousand times. I once saw the oddest thing—
how often does each announce this fact?

In the distant future, several at death's door
once more recollect this guy hacking at himself
and die shaking their heads. So they are linked
as a family is linked—through a single portrait.

The man's wobbly perch on the white tablecloth,
his open pants and strangled red chunk of flesh
become for each a symbol of having had precisely
enough, of slipping over the edge, of being whipped

about the chops by the finicky world, and of reacting
with a rash mutiny against the tyranny of desire.
As for the lunatic who was tossed out the back
and left to rethink his case among the trash cans,

who knows what happened to him? A short life,
most likely, additional humiliation and defeat.
But the thirty patrons wish him well. They all
have burdens to shoulder in this world and whenever

one feels the strap begin to slip, he or she thinks
of the nut dancing with his dick on the tabletop
and trudges on. At least life has spared me this,
they think. And one—a retired banker—represents

the rest when he hopes against hope that the lunatic
is parked on a topless foreign beach with a beauty
clasped in his loving arms, breathing heavily, Oh,
darling, touch me there, tenderly, one more time!

ROUGHHOUSING

Tonight I let loose the weasel of my body
across the plantation of your body,
bird eater, mouse eater scampering across
your pale meadows on sandpaper feet.
Tonight I let my snake lips slide over you.
Tonight my domesticated paws have removed
their gloves and as pink as baby rats
they scurry nimble-footed into your dark parts.
You heave yourself—what is this earthquake?
You cry out—in what jungle does that bird fly?
You grunt—let's make these pink things hurry.
Let's take a whip and make them trot faster.
These lips already torn and bleeding—
let's plunder them. These teeth banging together—
prison bars against prison bars. Who really
is ever set free? Belly and breasts—
my snout roots in your dirt like a pig
rooting for scraps. Arm bones, hip bones—
I'll suck their marrow, then carve a whistle.
Woman, what would you be like seen from the sky?
My little plane sputters and coughs. I scramble
onto the wing. The wind whips across the fuselage.
Who needs a parachute? Wheat fields, a river,
your pastures rush toward me to embrace me.

TOPLESS

At first I went just for the girls,
stopping by every six months for a few beers.
One liked to hang upside down as she stripped
off her clothes. Another attached matches
to her nipples and lit them. Good-natured
local girls and the music going boom boom.
Then they'd stroll through the all-male audience,
ruffle a few bald heads, rub against
some bellies, bounce on a couple of laps—
all for the dollar some fellow would stick
between their G-strings and oddly Platonic flesh.
One looked like an old girlfriend and even
seeing her fully dressed would send me tumbling back
to late nights in parked cars. But soon I began
speculating about the spectators. Many
were regulars, older guys in work clothes,
sipping beers, out of shape, skidding between
their first and second heart attack or stroke.
I was touched by the attentiveness of the girls,
their jokes and small talk. You know those
mechanical toys, wind-up rabbits or bears,
my kids have a couple, how they scuttle across
the floor only to end up in a corner, banging
their fragile tin bodies against the baseboard?
These guys were like that. And the girls,
in a small way, would set them straight again.
Just recently I watched a plump girl straddle
some codger's lap, hands on his shoulders, head
thrown back, prodding the guy with her questions.
So how's Billy, she asked, did he get a job yet?
And Betty Lou, did she decide to keep the kid?
While as she spoke, she swung her shoulders, left
and right, swinging her big breasts, so this guy,
with his chin poked directly between her nipples,

kept getting punched, left breast, right breast,
slapping across his face, knocking off his glasses,
banging his goofy grin as his head bounced back.
Not slapping any sense into him: too late for that.
Just one of the peculiar ways the world can plant
a smooch when you least expect it. How's the wife,
how's the back? How're the arches holding up?
Pow, pow—piston strokes from some bright engine
so that briefly the girl seemed the very center
of the world's own merry-go-round that had to be
just then whanging around through the night sky:
the colored lights, the spectral horses, the lions
with rubber teeth, and clinging to their seats
all these old guys, all the timorous and beaten
with their gray faces and ill-fitting toupées
and sappy smiles. Nothing bad at the moment,
nothing scary or mean; life without the sharp parts,
thrills without regret as the tumbledown music
zigzagged like lightning across the fretful dark.

SYRACUSE NIGHTS

"E agora, José?"—*Carlos Drummond de Andrade*

So your belly feels hungry
and your prick feels hungry
and you hit the streets because your eyes
feel empty and your hands feel empty
your days feel empty, a body
like tepid water and you want it hotter,
want each moment to beat faster.
Is this how it happens, my friend?
Forget the ardent embraces of your chair,
that your rug adores you and your bed
hankers for the heft of your body.
Your nose wants to sniff something,
your tongue wants to taste something,
your throat to drink something,
your fingers to argue, hands argue,
your feet want to whoop-de-doo,
while if your prick had a set of wheels
it would check out the town without you,
it would cruise the side streets without you.
Is that how you feel, my friend?
That the air dislikes you and your lungs
feel half empty, your belly half empty?
Where do you go when the town shuts down?
You are sick of books and the TV sucks
and you'd like to see one guy haul off
and smack another in the chops or watch
a girl strip off her clothes or have
somebody tell you what makes him fear
in that gray time before dawn or what
he loves or hates or makes him sad
or makes him stand up straight.
Is that what you want, my friend?
Aren't you afraid that people won't like you,
that the mailman won't respect you,

that the cops will come after you?
Fat people, thin people, Asians, blacks,
Eskimos, Indians, they've all got your number.
And women? Wipe that rope of slobber
from your chin, my friend. Try to calm
your trembling hand. Even a sheep
would look at you askance. You're
a suspicious character, an eager eater,
a subdivider of many pleasures
and you want it all to move faster,
the blood to move faster, the heart faster,
something on the brain besides this waiting,
this half-alert napping, the body hurtling forward
so fast that the wind sucks tears from the eyes,
a motorcycle on a straight road late at night,
tears streaking your cheeks, engine howling,
dark boredoms shrieking past on either side.
Heartfelt, brainfelt, bodyfelt, prickfelt,
rushing full tilt toward your personal zero:
leave a hole, fill in the blank,
I guess your guess is as good as mine.
Is that how the nights take you, my friend?

Straitjacket, straitjacket, straitjacket:
we are tired of this quiet life, tired of climbing
this mountain of pleases and thank yous.
It's time to kick a nun in the butt,
time to buy our prick a goddamned big car
and let the wind frazzle our ears.
It's time to stop this tiptoeing around,
to stop being the property of our property.
Who lives in this holy temple anyhow?
Let's get the formaldehyde out of our veins.
Let's strip this lampshade off of our head.
It's time to stand at the door, shouting, Come back!
It's time to welcome each of our badnesses home.
And here comes Envy sliding along on greased feet,
and gray-suited Lechery with his little cane,
and twin-headed Vanity winking into his own eyes,
and Anger going Grum, Grum on his little red scooter,
and chubby Appetite panting along behind the rest.
The beer's cold, the insults are hot. We'll dance
all night to the complaints of our neighbors.
We've got to get moving! Somewhere that shovel
stands propped against a wall, the patch of grass
is freshly cut where that final hole will be dug.
Let's march toward our grave scratching and farting,
our own raucous music of shouted good-byes.
Let's make sure they bury us standing up.

Had it worked well even once? Can one point
to a golden age of good times? Whatever
the case, the arms decided at last
to separate themselves. They were not

like the others; they had their own tastes
and ambitions: pleasures the others
could never appreciate. The legs went next,
alleging a life of agony within the community.

Hadn't they done the lion's share of work,
while forced to survive at the very bottom
of the human pile? Then the ribs went; the ears went.
The lungs extracted themselves and took the heart

because they needed a servant. The balls
appropriated the prick because they wanted
a bully. The eyes invited the nose
out of long friendship. Kidneys took the liver.

Leaving the tongue in the service of the lips,
the teeth marched off to their own village.
For a while everybody lived peacefully.
But then one heard that the hands had always

felt abused by the arms. And only the knees,
claimed the knees, knew what was good for knees.
If the feet felt downtrodden, then what about
the toes who left to form a community of ten?

And what about the toenails who without doubt
understood best what did best for toenails?
But after these further divisions, everybody
for a short time lived happily. Better not sing

if it meant being bossed by the tongue.
Better not feel, if it meant being beaten
by the heart. Better not lust, if it meant
being yanked up and downstairs by the prick.

But soon came additional discord—knuckles
could only be happy with other knuckles, hair
built its own hair ghetto, blood oozed in its own
private pool. Ponder the final drama of the teeth.

How could they have dreamt of life together?
Could the molars ever appreciate the true heart
of the incisors? Weren't the bicuspids destined
to live alone? And then the lower began to quarrel

with the upper, the left disparaged the right.
Stomach teeth, eyeteeth, wisdom teeth, baby teeth!
Consider the two canines faced off on a dusty plain,
stamping and snarling and beating their chests.

I was having dinner with my friends Howie and Francine.
The restaurant was old, maybe five hundred years:
whitewashed walls, great black beams on the ceiling,
no windows. We felt we were in the midst of history.
As Americans, the past seemed absent from our country.
The waiter kept knocking his head with his fist, trying
to explain something. The only words we knew were Pivo—
beer and Dobro—good. Hitting his head like that,
he seemed to be telling Howie he was stupid. First
he would form his hands into a circle, then he would give
his forehead a smack. The waiter wore a white jacket,
black pants. Perhaps he was twenty-five. Okay, said Howie,
sure. Bring it to me, whatever it is. This was Sarajevo,
the spring of 1989. A week of poetry readings, meeting
other poets, strolling with ice creams, attending the Saturday
night dance at the old hotel, no different than dances
I had attended in Iowa or Pennsylvania or Detroit.
Near the Princip Bridge a pair of bronze footprints
were set into the sidewalk. We each placed our feet
into these bronze souvenirs. This is where Princip stood
when he shot the Archduke and his wife. When the waiter
brought our dinner, there were our plates and on Howie's
plate a paper bag, like the bag in which a schoolboy
packs his lunch. Howie opened it carefully. Brains
in a bag, lamb brains cooked in a paper bag. We recalled
how the waiter made a circle, then knocked his forehead.
This was Howie's dinner. He was delighted. He could
barely breathe for all his laughter. We all laughed
and drank red wine. The other tables were filled
with happy people, men and women eagerly discussing
the subjects of their passions. When the door opened,
there was music from the street and a warm breeze
smelling of foliage and the dust of a thousand years.
There was the constant clatter of silverware on dishes.

The waiter laughed with us. He is probably dead now.
Killed by a sniper as he crossed a street or stood
by a window. The restaurant, the entire block, has been
transformed into rubble, so many rocks at a crossroads.
I've seen pictures in the papers. And those other diners,
those easy eaters, those casual laughers? Some
on one side, some on the other, some blown to pieces,
some shot in the head. Scattered, scattered.
But all that came later. On one particular evening
the waiter brought his tray with a paper bag on a plate
and we laughed. A fragment of that sound is still traveling
so far out into the dark, an arrow perhaps glittering
in the flicker of distant stars. Somewhere it still moves.
I must believe that. Otherwise, nothing else in the world
is possible. We are the creatures that love and slaughter.

She says she believes in reincarnation.
He says he's not so sure. Could the world
inflict such additional humiliation?
Could it ever happen like this? A black
woman is wheeled onto the stage.
She must weigh over three hundred pounds
but to hear her sing is to wander
lost in the center of a red flower.
Near the stage a blind man's German Shepherd
twists its head to the left and right.
A shred of something flutters between
those soft brown ears, not quite memory,
rather a scrap of residue, and the dog moans.
Could it ever take place like this?
Could it be that in other bodies, in another world,
the black singer and blind man's dog spent two weeks
in a cottage at the beach? Each evening at six
they drank martinis as they watched the red ball
of sunset slide into the sea. Afterwards, in bed,
the man thought of himself as a snail
working his way up the soft wall of the woman's body.
Now a certain residue remains: the red flower
of the black woman's song; the dog's brief perplexity
and grief, until the blind man touches a hand
to the dog's brow. Is this how it can happen?
Entering a room full of strangers, you notice
the dear curve of a forgotten neck; or turning
the corner on an unknown street, your heart
is caught up by window boxes overflowing
with red geraniums; or hearing the falling
notes of a song, your mind surprises the image
of the sun sliding below the line of horizon.
Is this what causes these unexpected oversweepings:
the sudden emotion, the confusion, then nothing?

PASTEL DRESSES

Like a dream, which when one
becomes conscious of it
becomes a confusion, so her name
slipped between the vacancies.

As little more than a child
I hurried among a phalanx
of rowdy boys across a dance floor—
such a clattering of black shoes.

Before us sat a row of girls
in pastel dresses waiting.
One sat to the right. I uttered
some clumsy grouping of sounds.

She glanced up to where I stood
and the brightness of her eyes
made small explosions within me.
That's all that's left.

I imagine music, an evening,
a complete story, but truly
there is only her smile and my response—
warm fingerprints crowding my chest.

A single look like an inch of canvas
cut from a painting: the shy complicity,
the expectation of pleasure, the eager
pushing forward into the mystery.

Maybe I was fourteen. Pressed
to the windows, night bloomed
in the alleyways and our futures
rushed off like shafts of light.

My hand against the small of a back,
the feel of a dress, that touch
of starched fabric, its damp warmth—
was that her or some other girl?

Scattered fragments, scattered faces—
the way a breeze at morning
disperses mist across a pond,
so the letters of her name

return to the alphabet. Her eyes,
were they gray? How can we not love
this world for what it gives us? How
can we not hate it for what it takes away?

HIDDEN WITHIN THE SLEEVES
OF THOSE DARK ROBES

If they had shape, how beautiful might be that shape:
needle fingers, old needle fingers,
capable of plucking a snail from its shell,
a hobo from his trousers, a saint from his goodness,
long of course but more like music than muscle:
perhaps like two tentacles of a giant octopus,
perhaps like twin roads rushing toward nightfall,
perhaps like the two dark roots of earth's white flower:
needle fingers, old needle fingers.

The child playing with blocks is building a wall.
He knows they are coming. The woman buying a skirt,
the man buying a truck, the other buying two canoes,
the one who hangs four gold chains around his neck;
the one who tries to hide behind kisses, the one
with books, the one who drinks, the one who fucks and fucks:
each one is constructing himself a wall.
See this man and all his accumulation:
a house in Florida, a house in Maine, cars
and Jacuzzis and three-piece suits. Hunted from the sky
he must be hard to spot, like an ant out
taking a stroll in tall grass, a single hard breathing
fearful speck tucked away behind all that merchandise.
Won't that protect him? Won't he last almost forever?
But then he is gone and his long cry fades into the ether.
Needle fingers, old needle fingers.

And my father, how we surrounded him at the end,
how we guarded the doors as he twisted and heaved
and kicked the sheets, his breathing
almost a panting, almost a crying out.
Was it the panting that attracted them?
Outside the night wind hurrahed the house, bullying
the trees, jerking at the windows. What's that noise?

A bumping at the outside door, a sigh, a scraping across the floor and something shouldered its bulk into the room and snatched him away. Wasn't our kind purpose enough, wasn't our love enough? Needle fingers, old needle fingers.

SANTIAGO: FORESTAL PARK

Teenagers and oldsters, married couples and lovers—
it is eight in the evening and everyone is kissing.
On park benches, on the grassy slopes of the hill,
sitting on curbs, joined in cafés they are kissing.

(I am not kissing; I am strolling along.
If I want activity, I have my newspaper.)

Why is the kissing so silent? Thousands of lips
jostling together and not a whisper can be heard
above the buses rushing people home to recapture
the kissing they have missed.
                              If I could be anything,
I'd make myself into an orchestrator of kisses.
Instead of millions of kisses snapped off at random,
let them happen all at once, a powerful smack
to rise above the roar of traffic, a smack to make
the generals glance up from their machinations.

Policemen, senators, dark-jowled funeral directors—
all jarred from narrow paths by the pedagogical kiss,
an explosion to hang like a pink cloud over the city.
It goes without saying people would change their lives.
I leave it to you to imagine how better we'd become.

My paper tells me the Year of the Monkey began yesterday:
a year of good fortune, a year bursting with happy babies.
I prowl through the park down a corridor of plane trees,
a gauntlet of benches and on each bench a couple kissing,
some are sprawling, fondling each other, heads on laps,
touching breasts, genitals, but always the silent kissing.

■ ■ ■

My solitude is like a big person walking by my side.
Some might say it is frightening, overbearing, cruel.
Nothing could be farther from the truth. See how
kindly it takes my hand as we cross the busy street.

This is common: two ancient buses careening
side by side down a city street at sixty
miles per hour. They are in competition—

different bosses, ambitious drivers—and they
hate each other. Two blocks up waits a clerk
at a bus stop, and the two drivers sneer and

shake their fists as their monstrous, lumbering,
smoke-belching aggregations of nervous rattling
leap over the cobblestones to snatch the clerk

from his patch of safety. As a fat man can be
pinched and bound around by a tight sweater,
so we are surrounded by imminent disaster.

Then, across from me, a diminutive old lady
rises to her feet. Her movements down the aisle
are like the downward flutter of a falling leaf.

The buses scrape together with a rush of sparks.
These are the occasions when life burns brightest
as the eager hands of death reach out to pluck

our living flower. The old lady sees none of this
(her mind is set on something baking in the oven)
and on the street no oddity is noticed: a normal day

with normal traffic. It is fall, the leaves turn brown.
We are ants clinging to a stone that one rambunctious
youngster flings into the face of another.

Among market stalls the pickpockets prowl
weaving within dark catacombs of canvas—
tables piled high with artichokes and oranges,
kerosene stoves, cheap sweaters, white socks.

Here my friend lost her purse, another his wallet.
Here men and women tired from the long week
spend Saturday in the labor of saving a few cents.
A man asks for a little coin for a bowl of soup.

His face and hands are the color of his clothes,
the same defeated gray. I repeat the pretty words
for hopeless: *sin remedio, sin remedio.* At the corner,
pickpockets warm themselves over a fire of sticks.

Turning their heads, their eyes comb the crowd
for loose pockets, for the hasty and forgetful.
And don't I desire a similar occupation?
Let me educate my fingers, let me practice

sliding ignorance from the mind, unhappiness
from the dark pockets of the interior.
Let me learn to pluck hatred from the heart;
let me sit among thieves and learn to steal.

FROM CONCURRING BEASTS
(1971)

(including two previously unpublished poems)

The poem as object; communicable; naked
as a mannequin after closing, stripped
between dressings, wig torn off, arms and legs
piled on the floor—the ability to rebuild,
a movement from nothing. The poem as bell
and the mannequin's head as clapper: a silent bell,
insistently proclaiming. Dogs stir. A cat
moves into shadow: now a jungle, now a tiger.
The poem at your front door at three in the morning,
leaning on a bell echoing in both of you,
which becomes both of you, coming together
from different directions. And caught by the sound,
you stumble downstairs; a single slipper and slap
of a bare foot; tugging at your robe; finding
the light which doesn't work. You open the door
and there is the mannequin dressed in dark silks—
a jumble of arms and legs for you to assemble;
its face white except for the mouth, a red river
between the ears; and the eyes which are empty.
And you would say something, searching for anger
beneath stones, some counterblow, some final
definition. But you wait too long and now your face,
at best never more than tacked on, begins to slide,
drip like a bad tap between your slipper
and one bare foot. And you would move your arms,
legs, but suddenly they are moving into you,
into your body like sleeves turned inside out.
You are unnecessarily afraid. There is no harm here.
You can refuse to accept it and in the morning
it will be gone and you will have forgotten it,
rearranged your face with a nail in the forehead.
You will leave your front steps as it will have left
the house you have opened to it and your wife with
her half smile and dreams of trees heavy with apples.

LEAVING THE BAR AND LOW LIFE AT CLOSING, I UNSUCCESSFULLY PURSUE SAINTHOOD

Keep your laughter to yourself, Dixieland band.
Uncle Charlie on the tuba has no time to wave
good-bye as, taking my change, I leave you
to your oom-pahs and amoral keys. This is my last
singalong. Sister Immaculata has passed the window
and I must follow on this stormy night where sirens
complain of nebulous somewheres. Yggdrasil,
the holy tree, still stands. The squirrel still carries
insults from eagle to serpent and back. Sister,
there's time for one last blast before the horn.
Slow your steps so I may reach you. We shall be
transformed and lunge toward sainthood like fish against
a southern beach. Odin didn't lose that eye for nothing.
The skirts of your dark habit turn a final corner.
Rejection is cheap when the town's shut down. Already,
the last taxis and cleaning women have run off
to their gray and nefarious garage. Rattle
those bones, Darkness, and eat another star for me.
I'm whistling Dixie among yesterday's litter.
Sister, where are your smiles and promises now?
Half the morning has been answered. No book or mother
ever told me there were streets like these.

IN THE HOSPITAL

He has refused absolution and moved piece by piece
into silence. His tongue lies motionless, disconnected;
there was nothing left to say. Unable to leave each other,
his hands nestle together, small animals, a joint urgency.
He will not stand or walk, there is no reason for it.
He has retired into himself, discovered the horizons
of corners and dark rooms. When they take him out,
the walls go with him, keeping their tight enclosure.
No food will tempt him. The nurses are white birds
he no longer thinks of touching. Sometimes he is
spoken to: it will rain; he can hear the thunder,
see clouds brighten and fall back. He shuts down
his fields, his dark barns. The thunder passes, leaves him
to his planting. He is aware of the sun, can feel
its benediction. There a tree, there a river, there a tree.

CONTINGENCIES

on Les Enervés de Jumièges
by Évariste Vital Luminais

There is a picture, a French painting, showing
two men on a raft over a river of light brown,
which is not mud but the absence of color
within color; beneath a sky drained of its blue—
water drained from a pond, blood from the body;
and the river moves between fields
which have been cut; trees aware of their dying
and no longer quarreling with it. The two men
lean back in the positions they find themselves,
and in their eyes it doesn't matter, in their legs
it doesn't matter. They have been hamstrung,
the old punishment. Their only knowledge
is the knowledge of water: the river moving
to the sea and the sea moving to accept their punishment,
now insignificant. Death has ceased to be an issue.
There is no memory of crime. There is only
the bare fact of landscape, the fatal lack
of possibility, and the end which is water.
Death is a small door opening through their eyes.

Sometimes, moving between two places—to class,
the store, to some person who seems to possess
the knowledge and cunning of light; and noticing
leaves drained and past color, the gray of concrete,
I think of this painting. And as I raise my foot
for the next step there is a slight trembling,
as if the Earth were resettling on its Nordic tree
or if the tree itself were twisting away
from the creatures that gnaw it. Suddenly,
I step into a world where everything is fragile,
leans toward breakage. Long cracks stretch
before me, paths of crystal leading
to or from the dark elms, the quiet of the sea.

For a short while my hands grow empty and nothing
will fit them, no stone or other hand. I become
a glass target among all things pointed and haphazard.

Two days of listening to a police radio
and everyone one around me is a killer. I have
walked this far, I must go slower. People
hang onto bodies that won't be with them
long. Their own and all the others.
Give me your hand. I hold it like liquid
with the same result. My own hand drips
like water from a tree after a short rain.
Green becomes the color of decay. The forest
surrounds us.
                    Standing on the fire tower
in the state park, I see a doe moving
beneath me. All twigs are pointed at it.
The ground can swallow it. If I shout
its sky will crumble. I refuse to breathe.
Nearby, hunters with bows and arrows rehearse
their comic lines: Who will grace our fenders?
Who will hang upside down in our immaculate
front yards? Their arrows have captured
the wind and its music. Their faces are like
drums, or clocks ticking. Their faces drip—
the noise of static on a radio. If I shout,
my own sky will splinter. Silence? I fill
my lungs like a swimmer diving to the bottom.

COUNTERPARTS

There is no sky today. Echoes of birds
worry their way northward. They must have
everything repeated many times. You are here
and elsewhere, your face breeding like fear.
It is not for nothing that I keep my hands
raised for the fall. This is a country of smaller wars.

You have your office and ranch house, your foreign car
and family. You are still not necessary. I see
your face in a photograph from the war, surrounded
by soldiers convinced by their smiles. Later
will be that look of faint surprise as you meet
the world and lie down to be counted.

The colors of blood are legion. Of necessity
your name must be also. Choose any direction
and it will lead to the heart. We call it a diamond.
Placed on the ground, we heap stones around it,
logs over it. What loss to a two-car family?
We bring flowers. In error, people will call it a funeral.

Days pass, fires must be tended—their flames
like small fingers looking for your eyes. You have
already torn them from you. All things desire
to be surrounded by stone. There is rain on my hands.
There is the steady thud of birds falling into hills
sloping with sheep. We memorize the art of decay.

A swift and pervading gray slips through my fingers,
cloud covered and accustomed to war. A bone
is my weapon. It may not have been mine. Each end
is sharpened and carefully aimed. The ground
and pine boughs hiss a warning. There are rumors
of summer. There are seasons no longer acceptable.

Having forced the peace, the Eskimos
are riding down to greet us, mounted
on great bears, gentle as clocks, legs
like the legs of the Statue of Liberty.
We will speak to them of seals, wallowing
in fish tanks, and convince them we are
pro-seal, pro-igloo, and will, in time,
be pro-Eskimo.

                 We see the first
high above us. His face like a nugget
taken from the hands of a drunken miner:
pitted, benevolent; then the others,
as warm as dollars waiting for our words.
Come to our houses, meet our daughters.
Let your bears make sport with our dogs:
our cousins half removed.

TEN FEET OF ROPE

Tight around my waist the knot,
looser at the post, the other end,
but not very. My grandmother tying me there,
to keep an eye out, she said.
I move from porch to road,
or sit, everything's gold
on the other side, sprouting and calling
my name. All morning I work at the knots,
by noon and free I'm off into fields
still unexplored, the danger's great,
I wear a sword, the rope follows me.

Later, the goblins defeated,
the black diamond found, I see
my grandmother come over the hill.
Pocketing the stone, I fly,
waving as I travel by her rage,
but she, unaware of wealth,
the thousand dead, or the princess
to be uncaptured by her lord,
steps on the rope, I stop short:
this was a beginning.

THE VELOCITY OF COWS

Standing there with Tony Sorce
in the dark garage, he looking
for junk, a found object
to take his name and run
to a new and well-lit place.
His straw has remained persistently
straw. He is tired of canvas,
the movement of space. I am a porter
and carry to my car the heavier objects:
a box, a wheel, the gray mansions
of mice. Words avoid my paper traps,
pass in all directions. Here
is the immovable, stretching
to scant fields, where I too
share the velocity of cows.

In the ungreased field they cling
to the grass to keep from falling,
so many shoes in a green box.
They graze, anxiously planning, touching
their backs in close conversation.
Two go over the hill, another follows.
In the high tower of guns and great lights
a guard shoots a short burst
to keep them from the fence.
They turn back. The fence is lined
with pheasants. There are no miles here.
At night, if the trucks don't come,
back to the barn, banging horns,
kicking soft hooves for company.

THE WAY IT GOES OR THE PROPER USE
OF LEISURE TIME

Now all my words are bricks
and I have built myself a small penitentiary.
I still refuse to be penitent but
take pleasure in diddling the idea.

If my cat continues to become human,
I will kill it and rid myself
of its echoes. The cat
understands this and will become more human.

Instead of barred windows, there are mirrors;
instead of reflections, there are doubts.
They wear belted and double-breasted raincoats,
sharp hats drawn over the eyes.

I have sent my cat on an errand of mercy,
a few coins and a note around his neck
to the Pope. My doubts tell me he is lounging
in a bar waiting for the King to die.

With an intense effort, I turn the bricks
back into words. They flutter and fall
like dying bats. Here is one called
Help, and another, Haste.

I refuse to accept them or see them as mine.
This is a poem about being alone.

EXPLAINING THE NATURE OF EVIDENCE

After the tables and chairs
voted to march on Pittsburgh,
the two rabbits grew a lawn
of their own and the barns waltzed
off through fields of ribald song.
All this happened yesterday,
and today I speak to you
about it. You sit, smiling,
roses growing from your head,
big black petals, grand pianos
with ebony keys. I sit,
talking quietly, my tongue
burning great holes in my mouth.
A gray Pomeranian
wanders in, bored and hungry,
looks once, then goes out again.
Your eyes soften. I speak of
the air pushing around us.
Somebody whistles, the black
roses turn in on themselves,
float off. I keep explaining.
You ask, what? You don't know who
I talk to, talking to you.

You sit as I do
but across the room.
Between us the silence
turns with the hunger
of great birds, their darkness
drops away at our feet.
Do not cry here.
There is too much space
for words, no bottom
for them to fall to.
We know the pit,
have carefully placed the stakes
with our own hands.

Becoming the river, we are the river.
Unable to accept it, we are drowning.
Your long hair floats on the surface—
sentences in a book I haven't read.
You ask for help. I can do nothing for you.
The river passes between high banks,
tree- and fog-bound. It passes over the tops
of intricate buildings. We can see the people,
but not their faces. They are shouting.
We can't make out their words. Fragments
of words float around us. We resemble
those fragments. The language is foreign.
We have waited too long for our decisions.
We have waited too long for the last boats.
We are afraid to surface or seek the bottom.
Insubstantial, we are not enough to cling to.
Foghorns continue their warnings:
the house is burning, the King is sick.
Without daylight, we have forgotten the sun,
accepted a darker place. Between the surface
and bottom, we may hang forever.

Ashes, the dissonance of unicorns: the edges
of my written name begin to curl, the ink
still visible through the fire. In absence of stars,
my natality card remains safely in Washington.
The sleep of animal counterparts: like frogs,
the consonants hold their sounds long after
the vowels have died. Poor vowels, asleep
in their boxes, dreaming of proclamations
and Latin verbs. The man at the top of the stairs
offers his assistance, keeping the silence of mice
orchestrating the works of Satie, the music
of children alone in rooms. He will gather
the seeds of new sounds, fit letters together,
making a puzzle of the United States, Vermont
lying buried in the deep south, all in his head.
A disbelief in unicorns and concurring beasts,
he fills their places, planting his sounds,
waters them, watches them grow, their blossoms
beginning to break forth jointly. The ink is gone.
Washington has wandered off the map. Somewhere,
in Montana, a bear, waking, hears his name,
shakes himself, grumbles off through fields
of flowering clover.

The justice of bells persistent in ringing.
A dark lantern emitting a single ray, one
red beam, sending it forth. Just
as the sun, dropping behind fences,
sends out its last light to fields
quiet with horses. There are too many things,
too much to touch upon. I have become an absence
and my name slides from the vacancies.
I have left my tongue and small list
of essential words in a locker at a station
surrounded by the old and poor
staring into their hands. If you speak,
I can only show you the key which is soundless,
point to the number which is empty.
There are no words. They slip from my fingers.
I see their fragments far beneath me,
flickering like candles about to go out.
I would learn to lie, speak only by number;
set wings upon the key and a small voice
to tell stories; to fly over the land, wrapped
in its mutterings, babble justice in the ears
of Mount Rushmore. Or I would keep a train,
small and electric; stock the cars with words,
fragments stolen from churches, schools;
learn the sly ways into your houses at night;
sing into sleeping ears of caves and rivers,
the death of trees, the silence of their dying,
the silence of the word as word.
There are too many things.
Repeat it to me: the justice of bells.
Then give me the sound and let it be
circular, going round with no knowledge of stopping.

Let a dark lantern be placed in the circle
and let me lie down by it, becoming
both entrance and exit of light. Let me
be the door and the lock. Let me
learn the ways of keys.

FROM GRIFFON (1976)

SIX POEMS ON MOVING

A Shout

I precede you in emergencies. I betray you
in dark places, killing silence. I can be
welcome or warning; dress in fear
or great joy. I have no preference. I exist
only in departure. I leave you breathless.

Wheel

I was the beginning. Now my children
surround you. You gave them your hands.
Now they have become you. You entrusted me
with your directions, forgetting I was a circle.
Steadily, I carry you toward your finish.

Sword

Carried, I am your decoration. Swung,
I become you. Born of earth,
drawn from fire, I am blamed for your troubles.
I am guiltless. You alone are the weapon
you are trying to put down.

Rain

I am nothing when not falling. Touching you,
I am cold. You may run from me.
Touching the earth, I change, changing it.
You may hide. Everything that grows,
grows from my body. You would die without me.

Arrow

I am a song until I stop. Stop me.
You trapped me, dug for me and cut me down.
Now stop me. You gave me to friends, brothers,
even enemies. Now stop me. I return you
to the earth—wrapped in wood, blind to the sky.

Crow

My color is the color of fear. My sound
is of a knife against bone. If I rest,
it is only to watch you. Flying,
I draw darkness behind me like a net.
Now it is over you. Now it is falling.

for Donald Justice

I am the giver of gifts, the bringer of life.
Everything you are, you are because of me.
You began to move, because I moved behind you.
You began to breathe, because I forced you to run.
I followed you. I tried to take your reflection
from mirrors, your shadow from the face of the earth.
Eager to escape, you learned touch
through fear of pain. Your own shouts
taught you hearing. I stayed behind you,
giving both warmth and light. Nothing was cold
except around me. There was no darkness
except with me. You received these things
because I taught you. You learned taste and smell
in order to know me. You grew older
in order to put time between us,
unaware that it tied you to me. Now
I give you the final gift. These wounds
are the eyes by which you see me.

Is it the night, you ask? Now you understand me.

The wind from the mountains is closing my doors;
it is time to begin forgetting.

    I'm sitting in a chair with a woman
    who is reading me a story.
    The story is green. It sounds
    like wind or morning light.
    I am the story she is reading.
    The woman smells of babies.
    I put them aside.

I begin forgetting like changing my clothes.
I have gone to a funeral: black shoes, black suit.
They smell of dust; I lock them away.

    I am in a hospital. There are nails
    in my leg. I shout into a rubber cup.
    I hang from the edge of a star, then drop.
    Two goats and the smell of ether fall with me.
    In the morning there is Cream of Wheat
    and a boy with freckles and stories of escape.
    I put them aside.

As I begin forgetting, I grow thinner.
Sadness is five pounds, pleasure three.
When I am done, I will be light or air:
something to see by, the draft that shuts the door.

    I stand by a bonfire. Chickens
    without heads run circles around me.
    Above me the body of a deer hangs
    upside down. Its stomach is slit open.
    I see my friends and family waving,
    calling from the belly of the deer.
    I put them aside.

. . .

When I am done forgetting, I will forget
my name, and priests will come and give me
a new one. Or perhaps I will have no name,
and when I am told what has been done
or not done, or when police come or men
with brittle prizes, I will say he just left,
never arrived, doesn't even ring a bell.

  I am in the kitchen. Something is baking.
  I take dry mittens from the radiator.
  The mittens are warm. There is the smell
  of fresh bread, shaving soap in the morning.
  A man and woman embrace in the center of the kitchen.
  The whole house is like red mittens.
  I put them aside.

THE MEN WITH LONG FACES

The men with long faces have come after my knives.
They put their ladders against the sides of my house.
They put their heads through my windows, all pressed together
like the spines of old books. There is much law within them.
My knives are taken and packed carefully in cotton.
How shall I be known from my animals without them?
How shall I keep apart the corners of my rooms?
The men with long faces speak of new futures and welcomings.
They ask my response, promising comfortable houses.
I grease my hands and the men try to shake them.
My knives fill with laughter like firemen at field days.
How shall I now read the night without them?
How shall I know which stars are lying?
They are carrying my knives to their wagons of boredom.
The streetlights come on and each one is singing.
Tied down in the back, my knives are forgetting.
How shall I know what is quiet without them?
How shall the darkness now keep its distance?

CLOUDS

The clouds moved in another hundred feet
during the night, just as they have done
each night for the past two weeks.
Now they hang barely beyond the range
of thrown stones. The sun is someone else's story,
the rich relation of a slight acquaintance.

Bending over us, the clouds have the texture
of faces seen through smoke.
Thoughts in a confused mind look like that.
Tell me again they are not hostile,
that they have come merely out of curiosity
to see again if we are possible.

If so, then why are doors more difficult to open
as if some sadness were leaning against them?
Why do windows darken and trees bend
when there is no wind? You call that occasional
roar the roar of a plane and I imagine
a time when I might have believed that.

But now the darkness has been going on
for too long, and I have accustomed myself
to the pleasure of thinking that soon
there will be no reason to hold on in this place
where rocks are like water and it's so difficult
to find something solid to hold on to.

THE GRANDFATHER POEM

John E. Johnston, 1878–1968

1

He is something he is falling into:
a body bunched around him like loose sheets,
old clothes too big for him. His eyes teeter
in their sockets. Bones keep the skin apart.
His face slips toward the mouth and would
slip through it if the jaw weren't locked.
He looks around the room like an animal
preparing to leap. There's no place to go.

The room's on fire. He points to a poinsettia
in red foil. Again he says: the room's on fire.
The horses must be gotten out of the barn.
There are no horses. There is barely a barn.
The years build up behind his eyes.
There is no present. Each person becomes a crowd.
I am a crowd. I see him searching through it
like a child at a fair. I call but he can't hear.

This is a dead house. Pictures of the dead
cover the walls. The roof is rotten. The porch
is caving in. Those who have died sit in chairs,
rest on sofas. In his own room, my grandfather
hunts for the present. I shelter in another,
reading family histories, stories of people
who die quietly in books, in a written silence
where I personally can turn the page.

January in Port Leyden, New York, and
I am here to watch a dying man. His hands
turn back and forth like stranded fish.
At his logging camps, French Canadian
lumberjacks called him the White Eagle.

I remember watching lumberjacks play tag
with bears in the Adirondack forest.
My grandfather's eyes keep sweeping the room.

The obvious questions have been answered.
Pallbearers have been discussed. I am to be one,
other grandsons also. The weight of winter has been
commented on and the bad behavior of cousins.
Now I am leaving. I take my grandfather's hand.
He holds it, refuses to release it. Startled,
I look and almost fall. His present surrounds him.
Everything topples toward his eyes.

2

A week later, driving north again with my brother
from Michigan, through Canada to the funeral,
we drive to the very heart of winter. Arriving,
we meet my grandfather's nurse at the back door.
She tells me to see my grandfather immediately.
The body is in the front parlor. She says he looks
so much better than he did last week. This is true.
He lies there like the poor memory of a healthy man.

Children run laps around the coffin, small
cousins, second cousins, some woman not seen
since her marriage in '39. This could be
a celebration or a sacrifice. Give praise
to the man who has gotten through.
We do not see him. We are still running.
Taking our neighbors' hands, we circle the coffin.
There is nothing in the center. This room is empty.

I want to shout: Let this be no surprise but
there is a dead body in this room, hidden beneath
rouge and powder, framed by that amazing
red silk hanging. Pinch him and he doesn't feel it.
Kick him and he shows true charity.
Lumberjacks come into the room, quietly and alone.
They are old and smell of whiskey. They look once
and leave, refusing to sign any book.

It would be better, cousin, not to have been
drunk today or at least not to be holding
that corner of the coffin on these icy steps
which have borne so many. Cousin, be careful,
or else our grandfather will give Port Leyden
a memorable good-bye when the box slips and twists
down the long hill to the center of town. Cousin,
will you put him back after he has made his resurrection?

We never buried him or saw him into the ground,
which refuses to accept the dead in winter.
We left him in the basement of the cemetery chapel
in what looked like a wine rack but held coffins instead.
Nine were there already, and the undertaker's assistant
swore that one had been opened. Just slide it in
and leave it. A wave of the hand and slam the steel door,
still echoing on what was never a funeral.

CROSSROADS

*They have married the ropemaker's daughter and
she is teaching them to fly.—Brothers Grimm*

Heights, I never climbed through windows.
Frightened by ladders, I robbed cellars,
the lower floors of houses. I stole shoes,
rugs, guilty secrets. My crimes were quiet.
I'd cut a man's throat only when he slept.
I was too fat to run much. Now the wind
lives in my hands and crows make me thinner
each day. I learn to fly in narrow circles.

Hidden, you knew me by the places
around me, places that I touched
and where now something was missing.
Caught and hung, I became a clown of air.
Secret, I was the hand in your pocket,
the reason your daughter came home crying.
Now I dance at the crossroads. Consider me
as you make the small decisions of your life.

Cold, all my choices were warm ones.
No gain could tempt me from the fire.
I robbed the warmest houses, took the warmest coats.
I worked in summer, burned stores for pleasure,
the blood of your brothers was warm on my hands.
I was hung in August, one of the hottest days,
only to become a signpost of winter.
These are directions you too must follow.

SEEING OFF A FRIEND

Early April on Broadway, south of Union Square,
a man jumps from a twentieth floor. I
stop him at the tenth. Tell me, I say,
what have you learned in your travels?
We sit and rest awhile. I have only
just asked the question, he says. The answer
will come to me later. He smiles shyly
and continues falling to the fifth floor
where I stop him again. Tell me, I say,
what have you learned in your travels?
He smiles again, being basically cheerful,
but shakes his head. These answers
are slow in approaching, he says,
perhaps it is too soon to tell.
                                    Beneath us
the crowd is clamoring for his arrival.
They shout and clap their hands in unison.
They would sing songs of welcome
if they knew them. They would beat drums.
I shrug and let him continue. He falls,
twisting silently. He nicks a streetlight,
smashing it. He hits the hood of a blue
Chevrolet, smashing it. He bounces thirty feet
and hits a parking meter, smashing it.
He lies there as people run toward him.
Their hands are open like shopping bags.
Their mouths are open like pits in the earth.
All his answers cover their faces.

SLOTH

from Grimoire
for Susan and Richard

If you were running, now you are
walking; if you were walking, now
you are sitting down. I enter
your body as sunlight enters
a forest after a day of rain.
You were on your way to a palm reading,
a new job testing Italian
sports cars, an axe murder. Do it
tomorrow. I am the cat rubbing
against your ankles, the hot bath
after an afternoon of chopping wood.
See me as a feather bed, red and
blue silk cushions in a warm room.
Lie down on me, lie down on me.
Whatever it was, it wasn't important.
Something about someone living or dying or
moving to Phoenix. Something small, no
heavier than the weight which now
presses lightly against your eyelids.
Close them. Tomorrow might be a hard day.

GLUTTONY

My stomach is the sky
through which the rain falls.

You invite me to your house for dinner;
I restock the shelves of my childhood.

Everything I eat makes me thinner;
I must eat faster.

I send myself love notes
and swell like a flower.

Everyone around me looks small and
insubstantial, like men adrift in a lifeboat.
I am the island they see in the distance.

ANGER

I am the simplest of disguises.
Putting me on, you fling yourself
at your victim. Taking me off,
you are the chance witness, finding
the weapon, just happening by.

∎

The animal within him is hungry.

∎

His hands come in boxes.
His skin is lined with knives.
His head is a mixture of phosphorus and
sulphur: strike him anywhere.

ENVY

You invite me to a banquet in your honor;
I bring my own dinner: ash and vinegar.

.

You won a prize
where I wasn't a judge.

.

I put on the news of your success
like a coat of nails.
Each step I take
is another reason to hate you.

COVETOUSNESS

Keep your toys and small possessions;
I only want your hands.
Everything I touch feels like it's mine.

.

He does his shopping in the houses of his friends.

.

I dreamt I was you, sleeping with your wife,
dreaming you were me, sleeping with mine.

VANITY

He lines the walls with mirrors,
floor and ceiling with mirrors.
He bows and blows kisses to the crowd.

▪

I write this,
you read this.

▪

His life story reads like a cookbook.
His telephone has two mouthpieces, no receiver.
He wears fur coats inside out.

SPITE

I steal your mailbox, leave
gum on your sidewalk. I
seduce your sister, ignore your wife.
I tear one page from each of your books.
I convince you that I am your friend.

■

When people ask about you,
I shake my head. When they
tell about you, I nod.

■

Today, I hang myself
from a greased flagpole
outside your picture window.
Yesterday, I stole your curtains.

Smart, stupid—let me tell you how to do it.
I could teach the rose about blooming, the porpoise
about swimming. I could write a book.
I could tell the dictionary about words.
Tightrope walking? Bring me a hank of rope.
Juggling? Just toss me a dozen eggs.
If you never ask, you'll never know.
Wherever I go, doors open like women,
women open like baby birds, men shut up
like clams out of water. I teach popes
about praying, generals about fighting.
Music? I whistle operas. Painting?
Let me draw on your wall. Poems?
I've just shown you how to write one.

for Pat Grant

ABSENCE

If these lines that I
see appearing on my face
were the lines of a map,
I would be with you now.

If the distance between us
were as tangible as the ice
that I feel, you would see me
sliding toward you, full of
joy at having found you, sorrow
at having been gone so long.

If my memory had the body
of a servant or thief
I would pursue it until it
returned what it had stolen:
already it blurs your face
with the faces of strangers.

Trying to remember you
is like carrying water
in my hands a long distance
across sand. Somewhere
people are waiting.
They have drunk nothing for days.

.

Your name was the food I lived on;
now my mouth is full of dirt and ash.
To say your name was to be surrounded
by feathers and silk; now, reaching out,
I touch glass and barbed wire.
Your name was the thread connecting my life;
now I am fragments on a tailor's floor.

.

I was dancing when I
learned of your death; may
my feet be severed from my body.

SILENCE

I am the music you were born to.
Then you put me aside, wanting your own;
like sticks scratching together, you wanted your own.
I am the song you will sing longest.

I am the clothing you were born in.
Then you changed me for bright reds and blues;
like a clown or bridegroom you wanted everything perfect.
Death is a marriage; you will wear me to the wedding.

I am the house you were born in.
Then you left me and went traveling;
like a child without parents or fortune you went traveling.
I am where you are going.

FROM HEAT DEATH (1980)

RAIN SONG

The woods are full of men with umbrellas—
the butcher from Roy's market, the mechanic
who fixed my car—they are looking for you.
They heard of a woman lying naked in the fields:
that was you. For days you lay in the north pasture
to encourage spring, as the sun touched your thighs,
your belly and breasts, and was at last so
disconcerted that the sky clouded over
and the president of rain took you for his wife.
You wore blue to the wedding; even the crows sang.
Now, hurrying through the trees, the black umbrellas
do not realize it is you dripping from juniper
and birch, forming puddles, then rivulets and
running downhill to the river flowing through town.
The people of Peterborough bathe in your body.
They drink glass after glass and say they feel better.
They smash their televisions and prepare to go dancing.
The fat town clerk and tax consultant, legions
of Republicans removing their clothes, baton twirlers
and firemen's band—all march naked through the street,
banging cymbals and drums as you touch them,
blowing their horns as you run down their backs,
tumbling at last into lascivious piles on this
rainy Sunday they will long remember but which you
have already forgotten as you flow down to the sea
into the stories of sailors and promiscuous fish,
and past that small promontory where I stand,
body greased and waiting for the long swim.

for Mekeel

OATMEAL DELUXE

This morning, because the snow swirled deep
around my house, I made oatmeal for breakfast.
At first it was runny so I added more oatmeal,
then it grew too thick so I added water.
Soon I had a lot of oatmeal. The radio
was playing Spanish music and I became
passionate: soon I had four pots of oatmeal.
I put them aside and started a new batch.
Soon I had eight pots. When the oatmeal cooled,
I began to roll it with my hands, making
small shapes: pigs and souvenir ashtrays. Then
I made a foot, then another, then a leg. Soon
I'd made a woman out of oatmeal with freckles
and a cute nose and hair made from brown sugar
and naked except for a necklace of raisins.
She was five feet long and when she grew harder
I could move her arms and legs without them
falling off. But I didn't touch her much—
she lay on the table—sometimes I'd touch her
with a spoon, sometimes I'd lick her in places
it wouldn't show. She looks like you, although
your hair is darker, but the smile is like yours,
and the eyes, although hers are closed. You say:
But what has this to do with me? And I should say:
I want to make more women out of Cream of Wheat.
But enough of such fantasy. You ask me
why I don't love you, why you can't
live with me. What can I tell you? If I
can make a woman out of oatmeal, my friend,
what trouble could I make for you, a woman?

SONG OF THE DROWNED BOY

Three oranges on a blue plate,
black loveseat on the cropped grass:
curlicues of iron; August afternoon,
small white clouds; pond surrounded
by a ring of birch, white rowboat half up
on the shore, clothes folded in the bow;
white hand below the surface of the water—
in the distance someone is calling;
fish break the surface, ever expanding circles;
a crow caws three times and is gone.

Lady of darkness wants a fair child;
Lady of cold needs someone to warm her;
Lady of water has taken me home.

THE BODY OF ROMULUS

The granular surface of the snow shines like parchment
in the afternoon sun as we stand on a hill above
Lake McBride. Beneath us several red snowmobiles
race across the ice. Parts seem unfrozen and we keep
pausing in our argument to wonder why the machines
don't plunge through into the December water.
For hours we argue about history which you say
is simply the story of great names and ignores
those others who suffered to keep them fed. But later
in Plutarch I read of Romulus and how one day he was
haranguing his people in a place called Goat's Marsh
when a storm overtook the sky turning day to night
and how people fled and the senators grouped together.
When the storm passed, Romulus had disappeared and
the senators claimed he had been lifted body and soul
directly into heaven. One even swore he had seen
Romulus taller and more beautiful than before, dressed
in flaming armor, and that Romulus told him he was
departing from Rome to become a god and henceforward
he should be worshipped under the name of Quirinus.
But Plutarch tells us that while the soul of a good man
is like dry light which flies from the body as lightning
breaks from a cloud, and while the soul of a wicked man
rises from the body like heavy incense, it is wrong
to think body and soul can be transported together
into heaven. Instead he argues that after Romulus
won his battles and established his city he became as
all men do who are raised by good fortune to greatness,
that he gave up popular behavior for kingly arrogance,
that he no longer maintained his office but dressed
in scarlet with the purple-bordered robe over it
and that he surrounded himself with young men
with clubs who carried thongs of leather to bind up
whomever Romulus commanded. And Plutarch suggests

that when the sky turned black with terrible
thunderings and boisterous winds from all quarters,
and when people fled and the men with clubs fled,
then the senators grouped around Romulus and slew him
and cut up his body and each carried away a small
piece in his bosom while rain carried away the blood.
And tonight after a day of argument I write this to say
that although the great names of history are given words
in books for you to believe or disbelieve as you choose,
to all the others are given the body of Romulus.
For Plutarch wrote that whoever becomes a despot becomes
contemptible, and wherever this may happen, even here
in this small Iowa town where the houses are like rows
of garden vegetables and sleep is an official sport,
even here the small names will trickle into the street
like small drops of water, and with them they will carry
tokens from the past: perfectly shaped fingers, bones,
pieces of liver, the bright blue eyes of the god.

FEAR

His life frightened him. The sun in the sky,
the man next door—they all frightened him.
Fear became a brown dog that followed him home.
Instead of driving it away, he became its friend.
The brown dog named fear followed him everywhere.
When he looked in the mirror, he saw it under
his reflection. When he talked to strangers,
he heard it growl in their voices. He had a wife:
fear chased her away. He had several friends:
fear drove them from his home. The dog fear
fed upon his heart. He was too frightened
to die, too frightened to leave the house.
Fear gnawed a cave in his chest where it
shivered and whined in the night. Wherever
he went, the dog found him, until he became
no more than a bone in its mouth, until fear
fixed its collar around his throat, fixed
its leash to the collar. The dog named fear
became the only creature he could count on.
He learned to fetch the sticks it threw for him,
eat at the dish fear filled for him. See him
on the street, seemingly lost, nose pressed
against the heel of fear. See him in his backyard,
barking at the moon. It is his own face he
finds there, hopeless and afraid, and he leaps at it,
over and over, biting and rending the night air.

A SEPARATE TIME

In the years since I saw you on Sunday,
I left my house and walked out across the earth
with only my occasional luck and knowledge of cards.
I met men and women constantly dissatisfied,
who hadn't learned to close their hands,
who sewed and patched their few words
fashioning garments they hoped to grow into.
There were winters sheltered in a cabin beneath pines.
There were frozen rivers and animals crazy with hunger.
But always I saw myself walking toward you,
as a drop of water touching the earth immediately
turns toward the sea. Tonight I visit your house.
In the time precious to newspapers and clocks,
only a few days have passed. The room is quiet.
Looking into your eyes, I become like an exile
who turns the corner of the last cliff and suddenly
looks down into the valley of his homeland,
sees the terraced fields and white-roofed houses
gathered on the hillside: then, the smell of woodsmoke
and a woman calling her husband in for the night.

MORNING SONG

Today, the pastures have dressed in their best grasses
    to parade past my window. They dress for you.
    Wake and choose among them.

Today, the sky which has been skittish all month, ducking
    behind clouds, seems to pulsate as the vein
    in your neck now pulsates when I lay one finger
    against it.

Today, the air, gathered in damp clumps, begins
    flickering with a blue light and there's a smell
    like a transformer gone bad; the hum of something
    at its dinner; the hum my bones make when you touch me.

Today, the snow which has turned a shade grayer each day
    contracts to a startlingly white cube, ten feet
    by ten feet, which strangers are already arriving
    to photograph. Sometimes your smile is so white,
    sometimes the white areas of your eyes.

Today, waking beside you, I saw the day had brought
    its best sky, air and circumstances to my house
    at the bottom of blue sky, and it seemed all this
    grew from your own white belly, and that I was like
    a poor gardener who stares up at immense scarlet
    flowers where he had thought to plant tomatoes,
    who stares at his hands, keeps turning them over,
    keeps glancing doubtfully over his shoulder,
    not knowing for what.

SONG FOR MAKING THE BIRDS COME

All winter you felt nothing. As your body
continued its necessary tasks, your sister,
the snow, remained keeper of your heart.
Now it's the first warm day of spring.
You walk out to the pasture. There's much mud,
and still snow on the north side by the pines.
You take this poem from your pocket.
Raising your voice, you read it aloud to the sky.
Soon birds begin to come, first the dark ones:
birds of anger, birds of despair. Then you see
the wren of friendship, the gray dove of hope;
then others of patience, joy and love's own red bird.
As you read, they begin to fill the air above you,
twisting and diving in great circles around you;
covering the poem with the sound of their cries
until poem and song become the same sound,
blending together under the warm March sun.
At last you emerge from the lethargy of winter.
Your heart is a great tree beginning to bud.
In narrowing spirals, careful descent, the birds
you have summoned arrive to make their nests.

for Shirley Stark

LETTER BEGINNING WITH THE FIRST LINE OF YOUR LETTER

Here the weather remains the same. Constant
summer sun. When was the sky anything but blue?
In the harbor park, boys on bikes plague lovers
and the pink-eyed dogs of the elderly.
Across the water, freighters take on cargo.
I stand on the shore, envying each destination.
Because you are not here, I think of you
everywhere; wherever they are going
they must be going to you. We were like
fat people in old cartoons who could
barely kiss for all their mortal baggage;
like holiday travelers who have missed their trains,
are stranded in a European station surrounded by
wicker baskets, belted trunks. We had such baggage.
It increased and became such a mountain that we
lost each other behind it, until our voices
grew distant and we returned to writing letters.
Whose baggage, whose mistakes, who cares now?
Listen, I am thirty-six, I have lived in
many cities and within me it is raining.
The deliberate ocean repeats and repeats.
Empty lifeguard stands, paper cups and
plastic spoons, the folded green cabanas—
all mark the deserted beaches of the heart.
Water drips from colored pennants, glistens
on the black taxis on the esplanade.
In the empty ballroom of a beach hotel, someone
is practicing the piano. In sitting rooms and parlors,
guests turn the pages of their magazines, look at
rain on windowpanes, look at watches, look at
the closed door of a dining room from which they hear
the rattle of dishes and silver, of tables being set.
Listen, from such a place I am writing you a letter.

Again and again, I try to put down a few words.
As day and sky dissolve in sheets of gray,
the sea repeats your name to the desireless sand.

FOOTSTEP

Each evening the man whose wife has gone
reads the paper with his back to the window.
She died in winter: cancer or a car sliding
wildly out of control—the cause doesn't matter.
At the hour when she often came home,
he begins hearing the footsteps of neighbors
passing in front of the house. Sometimes
one pauses, and briefly on the page before him
he sees her face as she looked on returning
from work or the store: cheerful and expectant.
The room trembles with possibility. Then the fact
of her death strikes him and once more she dies.
The paper goes back to detailing the forsaken
events of the day; the flowers on the wallpaper
return to their endless pattern; and the room's
air that had barely quickened seems dustier
as if it had been breathed too long, or
for too long had been unmoving and unchanged.

Now there is a slit in the blue fabric of air.
His house spins faster. He holds down books,
chairs; his life and its objects fly upward:
vanishing black specks in the indifferent sky.

The sky is a torn piece of blue paper.
He tries to repair it, but the memory
of death is like paste on his fingers
and certain days stick like dead flies.

Say the sky goes back to being the sky
and the sun continues as always. Now,
knowing what you know, how can you not see
thin cracks in the fragile blue vaults of air.

My friend, what can I give you or darkness
lift from you but fragments of language,
fragments of blue sky. You had three
beautiful daughters and one has died.

for Donald Murray

As a green thread winds through blue fabric
so this morning the sound of geese weaves
through the border of blue sky. He turns
past oak and maple gone golden, but sees only
a single crow heading north. In the pasture,
a man on horseback pursues three black steers.

In his dream it was a different house
and his friends were older: their faces
like fragments of bright light. A blue plate
had been broken and he searched among
the pieces, trying to put them together.
Through the window he saw the colors
of late summer. A feeling of falling:
then someone touched his arm. Light filled
the doorway and he seemed to lean against it.
These were friends he had not seen in years.

Returning to this town after an absence
of ten years, he keeps seeing himself pass
in cars, duck into stores, gathered with
friends around the tables of houses
he walks by at night. Half the streets
are torn up, half the buildings torn down.
He imagines who he might have been had he stayed.
At a traffic accident, he watches a man
twist on his stomach in the middle of the street:
the side of his face torn like wet paper.
Standing by the curb, he starts to call out,
then hurries away before the man can turn over.

One April in Ontario: a day so gray
that the lowering sky seemed intent
on stroking the earth. The air filled

with the sound of geese, and in wet fields
thousands of geese waddled, quarreled, stared
at the sky as flight after flight swept
over the fence where he stood with his friends:
a pocket of silence that seemed the very center
of the place the geese were coming home to.
That was eight years before and now
such a memory as to be something from a dream,
forgotten in the morning, then recalled
as he walks through the pasture and hears
the sound of geese going away, pausing
without knowing why, feeling a touch
on his arm, turning and finding himself alone.

SONG OF FOUR DANCERS

A path between two rows of pines; spring
smell of pine needles and dark earth;
gray stone benches along the path; morning fog—
he remembers her hands which moved like
impatient birds as she spoke. He remembers
the smell of her hair: wood smoke
and pine, and the touch of that hair
spun by some spider king. He remembers
the air that pushed from his lungs.
Some days later she flew to Europe. Twenty
years. Now he tries to imagine her
in one of the world's rooms, eating or
drinking, a life passed among strangers.

At the end of the path, four statues
in green bronze: four women in a shallow pool
dancing with raised arms. The fog breaks;
the sun glitters on the bronze. Kneeling,
she drinks from the pond, water
runs from her cupped fingers. Watching her,
he cannot imagine a time without her.

1

To begin with photographs of summer: lakes
ringed by white birch held by hands of white bone—
skeletons as delicate as the skeletons of birds.
To begin with a scene in a theater: a man and
woman sit on a red couch and between them
are photographs so bright that each becomes
a small lamp lighting their faces, making
a circle of yellow light around the couch;
but then it is darker, and moving back one sees
that the couch is alone on an empty stage.
The man and woman look at the photographs
and although they are talking there is no sound.
The only sound comes from a cleaning woman
at the back of the theater as she moves along
each row. She is old and lives with her cat.
She thinks of nothing but raising the seats
which she likes to flick up in such a way
that each snaps shut. Outside it is snowing and
almost dark. People hurry from office to home.
They are dissatisfied and all their cars
complain: snarling, honking, hating each other.

2

We sit in a parked car on an empty street
and I keep trying to talk but everything
in the car is shouting: the steering wheel
and dashboard, the pedals and black vinyl seats—
all keep shouting. Now your hands are pressed
against your ears and I keep raising my voice.
Cold night, cold street, rows of dark apartments—

then I see a gray dog run into an alley
carrying some creature in its mouth, something
that twists and raises its arms. And raising
my arms I turn toward you and abruptly
the shouting stops and the place where you were
sitting fills with silence. Before I can speak,
soften my words, you jump from the car.
Once, when you were away for a week, I wrote
your name on a banner to welcome you home.
Now the wind blows pieces of paper against
the car windows, and on each I see a letter
of your name, as if my voice were a pair of hands
good for nothing but tearing and breaking. How
did we become so foreign? I tell myself, I could
collect these fragments, patch them together.
I sit without moving as wind rocks my car,
whips scraps of white paper through the street.

3

A man and woman are being rowed out to sea.
Curved blades of gray water cut the bottom
of gray sky. She wears a red scarf and a thick
gray cloak. Their faces are red with cold.
He holds her hand, but through their heavy gloves
they feel nothing. Snow drifts down into the water
around them. With each wave, the boat lifts up,
then settles back farther from land. Their eyes
have not yet left the land: a yellow field
over which the sun is setting. On the shore,
a man and woman embrace, standing as one figure.
She wears a red scarf. They watch the couple
become smaller through snow and gathering night

until there is nothing but a red fleck on the shore,
until there is nothing but darkness and the steady
creaking of oars, until all they can see is a single
white gull where the scarf had been, weaving
back and forth on the night air like a hand.

4

I enter a room with a woman I can't
remember meeting. There is no furniture
and our feet clatter on the wood floor.
It is clear we will live here, that we will
begin furnishing this room and the house
that must surround it. Then there is a noise
at the window, and glancing up I see a bird
pressed between the glass and the dark night
behind it: wings fluttering on the pane,
claws making a scratching noise against
the hard surface. It rises, then falls back.
Behind it, tall pines struggle in the wind.
My love, the bird has your face. Its mouth
opens and closes. Its face is twisted
as if a hand around its body were squeezing,
like squeezing a piece of soft bread. I see
tears on its cheeks, and it seems to be
calling out, although I hear only the squeak
of claws on glass. The woman beside me
looks toward the window. What is it, she
asks, what is it? How can I begin to tell her
of our years together? I catch my breath and
wait and soon I will tell her it is nothing.
Cold night, cold street: my love, we had such
kind intentions.

Each morning the man rises from bed because the invisible
    cord leading from his neck to someplace in the dark,
    the cord that makes him always dissatisfied,
    has been wound tighter and tighter until he wakes.

He greets his family, looking for himself in their eyes,
    but instead he sees shorter or taller men, men with
    different degrees of anger or love, the kind of men
    that people who hardly know him often mistake
    for him, leaving a movie or running to catch a bus.

He has a job that he goes to. It could be at a bank
    or a library or turning a piece of flat land
    into a ditch. All day something that refuses to
    show itself hovers at the corner of his eye,
    like a name he is trying to remember, like
    expecting a touch on the shoulder, as if someone
    were about to embrace him, a woman in a blue dress
    whom he has never met, would never meet again.
    And it seems the purpose of each day's labor
    is simply to bring this mystery to focus. He can
    almost describe it, as if it were a figure at the edge
    of a burning field with smoke swirling around it
    like white curtains shot full of wind and light.

When he returns home, he studies the eyes of his family to see
    what person he should be that evening. He wants to say:
    All day I have been listening, all day I have felt
    I stood on the brink of something amazing.
    But he says nothing, and his family walks around him
    as if he were a stick leaning against a wall.

Late in the evening the cord around his neck draws him to bed.
    He is consoled by the coolness of sheets, pressure

of blankets. He turns to the wall, and as water
drains from a sink so his daily mind slips from him.
Then sleep rises before him like a woman in a blue dress,
and darkness puts its arms around him, embracing him.
Be true to me, it says, each night you belong to me more,
until at last I lift you up and wrap you within me.

for Peter Parrish

Shoebox upon shoebox—the elderly dawdle
at the backs of rooms; the middle-aged lean
from windows; the young rush in and out, in and out,
while cars collide like the applause of metal gloves.
All morning in my shoebox I try to write about a man
who moved from Connecticut to southern Maine,
bought a crumbling Coast Guard tower and now spends
entire weeks with a telescope staring east.
But each time I put down a word, a train
runs over it; each time a thought flutters
to the edge of my brain, a siren pins it
to its own blank page. Each time I imagine
this man from Connecticut seeking truth by hunting
just in one place, I hear a malevolent suit of armor
trample the cars, jostle the buildings, reach
into apartments and shout into ears that are like
dried flowers, like porcelain; and as I think of
this man I don't care if he finds truth or that
every day his wife and kids row back and forth
his limited patch of water with signs saying:
George is unfair and George is a creep.
I only imagine how quiet it must be in that tower
with the gulls crying of loss and violation
and the ocean slapping the beach to keep it breathing.
Outside, the mayor of this city is breaking bottles.
Outside, they have lined up ambulances,
fire trucks, police cars and remembering a sound
that once moved them, they try to play Beethoven.
Outside, the dogs reproduce their small replicas
of Rodin's *Thinker,* and pigeons hurl themselves
against the wall across the street because they know
the quick crack of their necks snaps my attention
from Kittery, Maine, where George stares out past
his wife and kids with signs and sense of betrayal,

stares east looking for and why shouldn't he find it:
some black freighter or *Flying Dutchman;* and George,
look, look, what's that pressing through the fog,
what's that raft of pine logs with two figures—
a tall woman in white with her hand on the head
of a huge Siberian tiger. Now they turn toward you
and both look so wise and benevolent that you're
sorry your wife isn't by your side so you could
take her arm and say: Hey, Honey! Hey, look at this!
Ah, George, the whole damn thing's a lie.
This is Boston, December, 1978. Now winter
sticks its hard body up the cracks of this city
and all my world is busting up outside.

In Copley Square, the derelicts sit side by side
on a stone bench. This one snaps and bites the air.
This one wears white spats and holds a black umbrella
between himself and blue sky. This one talks happily
to the empty place beside him as if talking
to someone he's known all his life. Those others—
their opposites, the sleek ones in bright colors
whom the city names successful—they keep
crossing the square and the derelicts keep trying
to catch their attention, not just for money or
conversation, but to prove themselves visible;
but they remain unsuccessful and nobody pauses.
Let's burn one. Let's stop fooling around and simply
burn one. Let's collect the carbon-colored clothes,
make a pile, light it and toss one on. Say,
the one with the umbrella or the one talking
to his friend the silence. Then the fire department
will come rushing up with five pieces of equipment
and they'll rush into the square and rush around but
they won't see anything, and one of the bums
will holler: There's a guy burning up on a pile
of our good coats. But the firemen won't see him.
Just another false alarm, they'll say and rush home.
Maybe there's one burning right now. Maybe
that's what the one bum is saying, the one
snapping and biting the air. Maybe he's trying
to tell you about the black smoke which you're
too dumb to see and his good friend, another bum,
blazing up on a stack of old coats in Copley Square.

PABLO NERUDA

Pablo Neruda stands on a corner next to a poster
advertising quick weight loss diet aids when I
happen by with half my creative writing class.
He wears a black boating cap and blue cloak draped
loosely over one shoulder, and he stands very still
staring at the clouds where he probably sees the profiles
of famous poets. At his feet lies a small brown dog.
We had heard he was dead and so are surprised and
walk around him several times. He has nice fat cheeks
and after a moment I reach out and touch one, but
gently and he doesn't notice. I look at my students
and I can tell they are ready for anything so I
take out my Swiss Army knife, open the littlest
blade and cut Pablo a tiny bit on the left arm.
He doesn't even blink but I think he begins to
concentrate more intently on the clouds. By now
my students are becoming excited so I open a bigger
blade and carefully cut a sliver of flesh from his
shoulder. I put it on my tongue and it's very sweet
with a faint taste of smoke. I chew it slowly.
Glancing at the sky it now seems a deeper blue.
My students see me smiling and licking my lips
and they too take out Swiss Army knives and start
cutting off small slices, although they don't stay
small for long, because suddenly we are ravenous.
It feels like I haven't eaten for days. I barely
pause to chew my food and I grow angry at my students
for pushing and getting aggressive over the more
succulent bits. One even eats the brown dog.
In practically no time there's nothing left but
a quickly folded pile of clothes on the sidewalk
with the black cap on top. Then we all become
embarrassed and won't look at each other because
we've eaten this famous poet, and even though he

tasted great and we could probably eat another,
and even though the city seems brighter and more
exciting than before, we still feel ashamed to have
surrendered so completely to such animal passions
so we point to our watches and make excuses and
stroll off in our separate directions, but shortly
outside a movie theater, I see one of my students
offering herself to the people waiting in line;
then I see another accosting a crowd at a bus stop;
and a little later in the lobby of a convention hotel
I see a third bothering the legionnaires. And you,
now that I have your attention at last, ignore these
imposters. They're too hungry to be telling the truth.
Feel this arm, this fat thigh. Why would I cheat you?
Even now the moon grows more swollen and the stars
throb deep in their black pockets. Bite me, bite me!

SONG OF THE WRONG RESPONSE

The poem is bare-chested, black and
shadowboxing beneath a streetlight.
In the rest of the city it is dark.
You're out walking your dog. Nervously,
you circle the poem. It turns toward you
and speaks of a disease of the heart,
perhaps anger. You can't make out the words.
Never have you seen a face so ugly. Then
it steps toward you and swings. You jump.
Still, it strikes you once above the heart.
On the sidewalk your dog is asleep. The poem
returns to shadowboxing. You are that exciting.
Once home, you phone the proper authorities.
Then I arrive and you describe the attack.
All next day you look at mug shots before finding
the right picture: a young man with some flowers.
This, I say, is a poem about love and
the difficulties of friendship. It is about
reaching out in dark places. The poem
touched you above the heart and you fled.
What happened in fact, you have forgotten.
What happened in memory will repeat itself and
each time you will act falsely and be afraid.

THE DELICATE, PLUMMETING BODIES

A great cry went up from the stockyards and
slaughterhouses, and Death, tired of complaint
and constant abuse, withdrew to his underground garage.
He was still young and his work was a torment.
All over, their power cut, people stalled like streetcars.
Their gravity taken away, they began to float.
Without buoyancy, they began to sink. Each person
became a single darkened room. The small hand
pressed firmly against the small of their backs
was suddenly gone and people swirled to a halt
like petals fallen from a flower. Why hurry?
Why get out of bed? People got off subways,
on subways, off subways all at the same stop.
Everywhere clocks languished in antique shops
as their hands composed themselves in sleep.
Without time and decay, people grew less beautiful.
They stopped eating and began to study their feet.
They stopped sleeping and spent weeks following stray dogs.
The first to react were remnants of the church.
They falsified miracles: displayed priests posing
as corpses until finally they sneezed or grew lonely.
Then governments called special elections to choose those
to join the ranks of the volunteer dead: unhappy people
forced to sit in straight chairs for weeks at a time.
Interest soon dwindled. Then the army seized power
and soldiers ran through the street dabbling the living
with red paint. You're dead, they said. Maybe
tomorrow, people answered, today we're just breathing:
look at the sky, look at the color of the grass.
For without Death each color had grown brighter.
At last a committee of businessmen met together,
because with Death gone money had no value.
They went to where Death was waiting in a white room,
and he sat on the floor and looked like a small boy

with pale blond hair and eyes the color of clear water.
In his lap was a red ball heavy with the absence of life.
The businessmen flattered him. We will make you king,
they said. I am king already, Death answered. We will
print your likeness on all the money of the world.
It is there already, Death answered. We adore you
and will not live without you, the businessmen said.
Death said, I will consider your offer.

How Death was restored to his people:

At first the smallest creatures began to die—
bacteria and certain insects. No one noticed. Then fish
began to float to the surface; lizards and tree toads
toppled from sun-warmed rocks. Still no one saw them.
Then birds began tumbling out of the air,
and as sunlight flickered on the blue feathers
of the jay, brown of the hawk, white of the dove,
then people lifted their heads and pointed to the sky
and from the thirsty streets cries of welcome rose up
like a net to catch the delicate and plummeting bodies.

FROM THE BALTHUS POEMS
(1982)

THE GREEDY CHILD

Gripping the mantel with thick fingers,
the maid's greedy baby reaches for fruit
in the glass and silver bowl. The baby
violently wants to become the fruit, to absorb
the fruit into his fat, transparent body.
A glass of wine stands next to the bowl,
while nearby the nearly full bottle is reflected
in a baroque mirror with an ornate gilt frame.
But the baby has no interest in the aesthetics
of his surroundings. Instead, he thrusts his hand
toward the fruit as if the bowl itself might
feel his desire and slide across the white marble,
allow the baby to suck it in, bowl and all.
Then he would tumble back, a round white heap,
and with puckered lips he would try sucking
the room toward him: he sucks and sucks until
bits of paper begin fluttering through the air,
until a gray hat rolls across the carpet, then
a pair of felt slippers, until the table and chairs
crash to the floor, begin also to creep toward him;
until the carpet itself pops its tacks and
the whole house starts being sucked inward,
until even people passing on the street feel a tug
as if a hand were tugging them toward the seemingly
innocuous street door of the house already half
devoured by the greedy baby just as a worm can
devour a pear from the inside, while the baby
sits on a floor as gleaming and polished as a plate
licked clean, and he bangs his little fists
and purses his lips, and sucks and sucks,
wants to suck in all the rich and tasty world.

THE CARD GAME

The boy has never known her not to cheat,
and kneeling on the chair, leaning on the table
as if preparing to pounce, the boy is preparing
to tell her. She holds out the winning card
and he almost refuses to look at it, keeping
his head turned from her. He knows she knows
he has seen her cheating, knows she doesn't care.
He knows she thinks that were he to accuse her,
he would become so angry he'd tear up the cards,
knock over the table and chairs. He might even
hit her, but instead he looks sullen and turns
half away, while she cheats and he wishes he could
break her the way he used to break her toys.
Around them, the tall green hedge seems to press
down upon them, while in the city beyond the hedge
their neighbors rob and despise each other, and in
the city beneath them rats scurry through pipes
squeaking and leaping at each other, biting and
bullying one another. At last the boy reaches to
accept the card, allows himself to be beaten as she
already knows he will do. And what has she won?
What will she take from this brother she loves?
She will place his moon face in the sky to watch
over her, keep his cat body nearby to protect her.

THE LIVING ROOM

Sunday, mid-afternoon, radiator pipes knocking
and the air thick with dry heat. Propped on one elbow,
a girl leafs through a book of photographs lying
on the yellow rug before her. She is bored and, kneeling,
she resembles a cat edging its way through tall grass.
Behind her is the piano she has just stopped playing,
practicing the waltz she has spent the day learning:
the waltz her mother sometimes plays, and with which
she will surprise her parents when they return home.
On the green couch, her blond sister half sleeps,
arm outstretched along the curved mahogany back.
In the near silent room, the girl on the couch still
hears the waltz her sister has practiced over and over,
but now it seems the music comes from the orchard where
all morning she helped gather apples. With eyes shut,
she sees her parents together, but younger and happier
than she has known them: her parents as she has seen them
in old photographs, before sickness and war and the deaths
of their own parents—her mother in a long red coat,
her father wearing a crushed felt hat lost years ago—
walking with their heads inclined toward one another,
almost touching as they talk quietly. The girl wants
to call to them, to make some sign, then she realizes
that from her own body comes the sound of the waltz,
but now almost languorous, almost sad as the man and woman
ascend the hill through the orchard: Cortland, Macoun, Rose
of Caldaro, Autumnal Gray Rennet, Baldwin, Abundance—
and her parents' thin shapes among heavily laden trees.

GETTING UP

The cat with yellow eyes doesn't yet realize
the bird is made from paper and wood. Hesitating
at the edge of its basket on the bed, the cat
stares at the toy bluebird in the girl's hand.
The girl wants to know what it's like to kill,
wants to see the cat embarrass itself, then start
washing itself. She leans back on white pillows,
white sheets, one foot just touching the floor.
She is naked and holds the bird in her right hand;
with her left she coaxes the cat, encouraging it
to leap as she watches intently with narrowed eyes.

Around her, she hears the house stirring with
morning activity: a smell of coffee from the kitchen,
a door slamming and her father's feet on the stairs.
Soon she must get up, dress for school in her
blue skirt, white blouse. Her father will drive her
on his way to work, while she finishes a report
on Argentina and its exports. Once at school,
she will join her friends, all dressed as she is,
and together they will proceed through the civilized
unwinding of their day. But now, naked with her cat,
she is learning about death and the desire
to kill; she is learning about humiliation and
the manipulation of power; and it's as if
the entire day ahead were a great inverted
pyramid resting on its tip upon these few seconds,
as the girl waits, her lips parted in a half smile,
and the cat takes a half-step, preparing to leap.

THE GUITAR LESSON

Hand gripping the girl's thigh, pressed nearly upon
what her Bible calls her loins, the girl's music teacher
tries to make her sing. But she will not sing.
She will not play the piano nor even the guitar.
Stretched on her back across the woman's knees,
blue skirt yanked past her navel, the girl pretends
to be asleep, while with her left hand she tugs
at the top of her teacher's gray dress, freeing
the right breast which flops out above her and so
startles the girl she nearly cries out, but she
won't cry out, won't sing, won't play the guitar.
She hates those black notes on the page: the snappy
little eighth notes, self-important whole notes.
Who says she must start at the beginning
and proceed to the end? She wishes to play only
the middles of songs, sing only the half notes—
and so she and her teacher have come to quarrel.

Now her teacher's white breast hangs above her,
as round as a whole note, and the girl knows she
could sing that note if she chose, and her teacher
would be blown away as if by a singing tornado.
The girl thinks of the songs she sings to her dog
or the sounds she makes like quacking like a duck.
Her teacher hates it when she quacks like a duck.
For that matter, the girl hates the way her teacher
takes her nice fat songs and trims them to fit
black marks on a page. So she closes her eyes
and pretends to sleep, while her teacher
pulls her hair. The girl doesn't care.
In her mind, she sketches a picture of a mountain.
Then she places herself at the top, wearing
her best blue skirt, red jacket. The girl looks
to the east where the sun is impatient to rise.

So she clears her throat and begins to quack grandly
and the sun climbs into the sky like a fat shopper
on a jerky escalator, for which she thinks her music
teacher and all the tuneless world should thank her.

THE ROOM

Either it's her sister or an apparition, and she hopes
it's the latter, but she expects it's her sister pretending
to be invisible, since she recognizes her sister's
red socks and slippers. Otherwise the figure is naked
except for the white towel draped over one shoulder.

Kneeling by the fireplace, the girl is torn between speaking
or continuing to read her book. If she speaks, she must deal
with her sister's petulant sense of failure, yet if she
keeps quiet she must endure her sister's boasting after
parading about in a state of false invisibility.

So, despite the red socks, the girl decides it must be
an apparition, and since she has been reading about Rome
she decides the figure is an androgynous Roman
who has arrived to address the Senate on the fate of
hermaphrodites everywhere. From her place on the rug,

the girl finds androgyny more interesting than the phony
invisibility of her sister who is a year older and on the edge
of becoming a woman. The girl hasn't decided what she
thinks about becoming a woman, but knows androgyny and
invisibility are poor second choices. What she feels,

almost without knowing it, is that her own choices
have become fewer. It seems not long before that
the world around her—animals, weather, even the people
on city streets who shove and bump one another—
that every waking hour offered endless opportunity.

But now she speculates on a future in which each year
the world resumes possession of all she has borrowed,
takes back blessings she thought were hers to keep,
until she too becomes an apparition, less than invisible,
without book or Roman Senate or big sister to amuse her.

THE MOUNTAIN

Who does the mountain belong to anyway? As Wordsworth
believed all mountains belonged to him, so these
seven people think it belongs to each of them alone.

To the left, a young man with pipe and backpack
kneels and sticks his staff hard against the rock
like a sword to a Saracen neck. In kneeling,

he copies the contours of the pinnacle behind him,
and he's of the opinion this constitutes possession.
But beside him the beautiful blond girl disagrees

as she lifts her joined hands into sunlight, mimicking
the masculine shapes of jutting rock, believing
such sympathy makes her mistress of all she surveys.

On the ground at right, a girl in a red coat pretends
to sleep, her body imitating the gentle slope, while
with her ear to the earth she hears a faint whispering

promising to love her alone. Behind her a young man
recites poetry to the stone outcropping he would
like to become. What kind of poetry? Take a guess:

Peruvian or Swiss. A little farther an old couple dawdles
at the cliff's edge. The man points to where his trucks
will remove the mountain, as his wife holds her straw hat

and nods. They plan to rebuild all this in the backyard
of their suburban home, unaware the mountain is rebuilding
them into the slight hill rising to the cliff beyond them.

Who does the mountain belong to? Rather, to whom do these
seven people belong? Only the seventh is formulating
an answer, as far to the right he climbs steadily faster—

a small figure in a white shirt, black vest. He's happy
to be alone, persuades himself that he hates people
and hopes someday to be as misanthropic as rock—

even though he desires the blond girl thrusting herself
upward in mannish postures. But he wants to think it's like
desiring himself: like walking to the top of the mountain

is like walking to the top of himself. As he climbs,
he digs his heels firmly into the rock, and feels
the pain the mountain must feel as if it were his pain.

Briefly, he looks back toward the others, to the girl
lifting her arms into blue sky—his mountain, his sky—
and he tries to see them all as fragments of himself,

see them as images of his own imagination, and he reaches
the conclusion there never was a mountain, that he is
sitting in his small room in the city, watching the wall

across the alley; and every day he grows more afraid of how
alone he is, yet he refuses to ask anything of anyone:
that like a mountain he will ask nothing of all the world.

THE TRIANGULAR FIELD

In bright morning sunlight, the horse appears pink,
and the man is so pleased to see it that he waves
as he walks toward it across the triangular field.
The horse glances up from between two apple trees
and waits. The man was awakened early by dreams of
winter and self-doubt, dreams of no money in the bank;
and now he wants to clear his head by galloping bareback
through summer lanes with dust billowing around him,
light flickering around him in a hundred shades of green.
And he decides to gallop so fast that all the impediments
and small debts of his life will be lost in a swirl
of debris, that even his own death which he thinks
must be as gnarled as the trunks of surrounding trees
will be left deserted and discouraged in the middle
of some sun-choked lane.
                            As he walks toward the horse,
he anticipates the swell of its body beneath him,
pushing out his thighs as he lies with heels pressed
against its belly, urging it to gallop even faster.
And he's sorry he can't take this back to the city:
simply, the flickering light and smell of summer grasses.
Then, in winter, when he and the world fought one another
and he gnawed at himself, was cruel to people around him,
he would think of the morning he galloped the pink horse
between apple trees, and the world fitted together
without angry words and extra pieces, and across
the lurching sky he saw his own name hastily scrawled
as if on an IOU from somebody notoriously disreputable,
someone who has never been known to tell the truth,
but who for the brief moment he has chosen to believe.

THE WHITE SKIRT

For an hour he wonders what the girl could be thinking
as she sits in the green armchair with her head
slightly lowered, her thick red hair slightly
falling forward. She has unbuttoned her white blouse
and her breasts hang loosely in the halter of her slip.

The man watches from the balcony of an apartment next door.
Strings of Christmas lights dangle between palm trees.
Through the open French windows, the man considers how
the girl stares at some spot on the floor to the right
of her red slippers, the elaborate folds of her white skirt.

Next to him, a neighbor complains that his wife and children
don't love him, while inside the man watches his own wife
dancing with their host: one fat hand massaging
the small of her back. The man would like to go home,
but senses the emptiness of his house waiting for him.

Now he notices how the girl's bare arms hang loosely
over the arms of her chair, that her whole body is limp
as if she'd been dancing all night; as if her lover
had just left her to move to another city; as if
in the fact of her beauty, she also beholds her own

mortality which will at last fall across whatever
she may be doing in the way a curtain can fall
across a sunlit window. The man again considers
how silent his own house must be, like the silence
inside an empty suitcase or empty suit of clothing.

Abruptly, he stands up, leaves the apartment without
speaking to his wife. He feels his life evading him,
slipping past like a puff of air between open fingers.

Once outside he seeks out the lights of the girl's window,
sees the lights of the party he has left. Down the street

he sees the darkness of his own house. He wants to knock
at the girl's door, find the words to change their lives.
Then he pauses. For every action he can imagine taking,
he imagines reasons for not taking it; for every gain,
he imagines all the losses. He takes a few steps toward

the girl's building, then a few steps back. It's the dance
he has become best at. Gnawing and arguing at himself,
he remains standing as lights blink out in the windows
around him, until his wife finds him and without speaking
grips his arm, draws him down to his own dark home.

GOTTÉRON LANDSCAPE

The stark rock bulk of Gottéron ravine rises
into autumn sky, topped by a black row of pines
whose tips jut like sawteeth against the charcoal
gray darkness. Winding across the bottom,
like a flea on a chin, a man carries a bundle
of firewood along a path above the boulder-
interrupted stream. To someone watching from
the opposite hill, the man would be invisible
if it weren't for bare branches of aspen and
birch which appear to point toward him. Even
the rocks seem to gesture toward him as if
rock and rushing water were preparing to sweep him
from the path into the massive autumn night.
Bearing a bundle of sticks as big as his body,
the man is unaware of being particularly
heroic in pursuing the details of his life
while on the verge of being swept away by
the details of the world around him. He has never
thought himself as one of the world's brave men.
He thinks only that he has been walking a long time,
that he is hungry and the wind bites his cheeks.
He thinks of the fire in his kitchen and the stew
his wife has promised him. As the man climbs the path
above the stream, he can almost smell the garlic
and thick gravy, see the fat white potatoes,
as if their warmth made a kind of light or even
a length of fine silk thread he can barely grip
between cold fingers but which step by perilous step
winds him home through the rock bulk of Gottéron ravine.

KATIA READING

The book is golden with an orange spine, and the girl
reading leans back in her chair, one leg outstretched,
the other tucked up: one foot on the edge of the seat.
Because of her short red skirt and purple halter,
her bare legs and feet, you decide the room is hot,
that it's a midsummer evening. But the girl reading
has forgotten the evening, the house around her,
the city beyond her, has forgotten her small body
tucked into her chair. Instead, she is encompassed
by her book in the way one is surrounded by a sunlit
summer morning, except her head is turned slightly
to one side as if she found the page too bright.

All this is a painting you have seen often, and often
you have wondered what the girl is reading. At first
you thought her book was something frightening:
the way her head is turned from the page,
the way she has forgotten the presence of her body.
It is a long thin book, too thin for a novel;
and you have come to think it must be poetry.
Seeing her makes you remember the first time
you read a poem that moved you, not even realizing
it was a poem, but feeling you saw yourself on the page;
saw yourself with nothing to redeem you, as a creature
who wears his body like an ill-fitting suit of clothes.

Perhaps you would have laid aside your book,
but so completely was the world lifted out of
its daily banality that you kept on reading.
What had your world been until then? First you
ate something, then you bought something, then you
went bowling; a world where men passed their lives
peering under the hoods of cars. And like the girl
in the painting you must have turned your head

slightly as if from a loud noise, and you too became
like someone who has left on a journey, someone who
has become the answer to his own impossible riddle:
who condemned to a room is at last free of the room.

THE WINDOW

The woman who is waiting for the evening draws
a black line over one eyebrow, then rises from
her dressing table, walks to the gramophone.

Immediately, the tremulous voice of Ada Falcon
singing "Garden of Desire" fills the room
like a perfume whose smell slides over the walls,

over the table by the window and into the autumn
afternoon, crosses the street and drifts through
the top story of a retired clerk who sits

in his slippers at a table shuffling cards. His
wife is making cabbage soup and all day that smell
has filled his life. Now the tango draws him toward

the window where in the street he sees two children,
perhaps six or seven, poised cheek to cheek, their
joined hands thrust forward like the prow of a ship,

who remain motionless as the woman on the record
sings about loss. As he listens, the clerk recalls
dances he attended as a young man, thinks of a dance

at the seashore where he had gone with his parents.
The dance floor was a pier over the water and pines
along the shore swayed in a summer wind. Standing

at the window, the man begins to see strings of
colored lights, the band in white shirts with blue
ruffles on the sleeves. He tries to picture the faces

of the girls, but sees only a style of hair, a ribbon;
smells the mixture of perfume and sweat; sees the ocean
with whitecaps emerging like messages from the dark.

• • •

He assumed he would someday cross that ocean,
win for himself a life of wealth and excitement—
all the things that never happened, for his life

took other unexpected turnings: a job in an office,
illness, a childless marriage, days falling around him
like scattered cards, bringing him at last to this

small apartment on a small street where his life
seems wrapped in the smell of cabbage soup.
Looking down at the boy and girl poised motionless

in the street, the man wants to call to them.
But what could he say? Instead, he turns aside as
the children take one step, then another, hearing

only the music as their feet stumble forward,
gripping each other tightly as they spin and dip.
Look, they say, see how gracefully we are dancing.

JAPANESE GIRL WITH RED TABLE

The Japanese girl thinks she will die today.
In her mirror, she sees she is already dying
and she tries to compose her face into how
it will appear in death: forgiving, forgetful.
Between her white breasts, she already sees
the red mark of the knife—red as the red table
on the floor behind her, red as the red border
of the purple robe falling open around her
as she kneels before her mirror. Yes, she thinks,
she will destroy herself today; and her lover,
who has not come, will hear of it from people
crying to each other as he passes on the street
with his destination a solid object in his mind,
as real as the red table or the black and white
vase upon the table. He will hear that a girl
has been found with a knife in her breast,
but he won't believe it's she as he continues
toward the red table in his mind. Then at last
some friend will bring him the news, tell him
while he sits with his wife in the early evening,
eating sweets and drinking tea as he describes
the small business of his day. He will be holding
a porcelain cup with a picture of a single gull,
and he will listen to how a girl has been found
lying naked in her own blood on the golden rug
he gave her, while within him the words will be
eating his body as fire eats paper, as he tries
hopelessly to hold his cup steady and make no face.

THE STREET

Across the street, the carpenter carries a golden
board across one shoulder, much as he bears the burdens
of his life. Dressed in white, his only weakness is
temptation. Now he builds another wall to screen him.

The little girl pursues her bad red ball, hits it once
with her blue racket, hits it once again. She must
teach it the rules balls must follow and it makes her
quite wild to see how it leers at her, then winks.

The Asian couple wants always to dance like this:
swirling across a crowded street, while he grips
her waist and she slides to one knee and the music rises
from cobblestones: some days Ravel, some days Bizet.

The departing postulant is singing to herself. She
has seen the world's salvation asleep in a cradle,
hanging in a tree. The girl's song makes
the sunlight, makes the breeze that rocks the cradle.

The baker's had half a thought. Now he stands like a pillar
awaiting another. He sees white flour falling like snow,
covering people who first try to walk, then crawl,
then become rounded shapes: so many loaves of bread.

The baby carried off by the heartless mother is very old and
for years has starred in silent films. He tries to explain
he was mistakenly exchanged for a baby on a bus, but he finds
no words as once again he is borne home to his awful bath.

First the visionary workman conjures a great hall, then
he puts himself on the stage, explaining, explaining:
where the sun goes at night, where flies go in winter,
as attentive crowd of dogs and cats listen in quiet heaps.

Unaware of one another, these nine people circle around
each other on a narrow city street. Each concentrates
so intently on the few steps before him, that not one
can see his neighbor turning in exactly different

yet exactly similar circles around them: identical lives
begun alone, spent alone, ending alone—as separate
as points of light in a night sky, as separate as stars
and all that immense black space between them.

FROM BLACK DOG, RED DOG
(1984)

THE GUN

Late afternoon light slices through the dormer window
to your place on the floor next to a stack of comics.
Across from you is a boy who at eleven is three years
older. He is telling you to pull down your pants.
You tell him you don't want to. His mother is out
and you are alone in the house. He has given you a Coke,
let you smoke two of his mother's nonfilter Pall Malls,
and years later you can still picture the red packet
on the dark finish of the phonograph. You stand up
and say you have to go home. You live across the street
and only see him in summer when he returns from school.
As you step around the comics toward the stairs,
the boy gives you a shove, sends you stumbling back.
Wait, he says, I want to show you something.
He goes to a drawer and when he turns around
you see he is holding a small gun by the barrel.
You feel you are breathing glass. You ask if it is
loaded and he says, Sure it is, and you say: Show me.
He removes the clip, takes a bullet from his pocket.
See this, he says, then puts the bullet into the clip,
slides the clip into the butt of the gun with a snap.
The boy sits on the bed and pretends to study the gun.
He has a round fat face and black hair. Take off
your pants, he says. Again you say you have to go home.
He stands up and points the gun at your legs. Slowly,
you unhook your cowboy belt, undo the metal buttons
of your jeans. They slide down past your knees.
Pull down your underwear, he tells you. You tell him
you don't want to. He points the gun at your head.
You crouch on the floor, cover your head with your hands.
You don't want him to see you cry. You feel you are
pulling yourself into yourself and soon you will be
no bigger than a pebble. You think back to the time
you saw a friend's cocker spaniel hit by a car and you

remember how its stomach was split open and you imagine
your face split open and blood and gray stuff escaping.
You have hardly ever thought of dying, seriously dying,
and as you grow more scared you have to go to the bathroom
more and more badly. Before you can stop yourself,
you feel yourself pissing into your underwear.
The boy with the gun sees the spreading pool of urine.
You baby, he shouts, you baby, you're disgusting.
You want to apologize, but the words jumble and
choke in your throat. Get out, the boy shouts.
You drag your pants up over your wet underwear and
run down the stairs. As you slam out of his house,
you know you died up there among the comic books
and football pennants, died as sure as your friend's
cocker spaniel, as sure as if the boy had shot your
face off, shot the very piss out of you. Standing
in the street with urine soaking your pants, you watch
your neighbors pursuing the orderly occupations
of a summer afternoon: mowing a lawn, trimming a hedge.
Where is that sense of the world you woke with
this morning? Now it is smaller. Now it has gone away.

BIRTH REPORT

The week the nuclear protesters stormed the gates
of the Seabrook plant was the same week you were born.
The protesters were repelled. You spent thirty hours
being forced from your mother's body, while I filled
sheets of yellow paper charting the length of each pain.
The week of the first snow was the week you were born.
The week the Pope packed Yankee Stadium. The week of the first
stories of people freezing to death due to the cost of oil.
In bright light, I watched your head ease itself out of
my wife's vagina: your scalp blue, flecked with blood.
The week of the World Series and new boredoms on television.
The week politicians maneuvered election year mileage
out of Russian troops in Cuba. The week a racist
from Philadelphia gave me three dollars for your
future and warned you to stay out of Philadelphia.
I took you and bathed you in a plastic tub in the first
seconds of your life, while you twisted and cried; and
outside the world lunged and snapped at the hospital door,
and trees turned color; and corporate business tried
to make certain you would inherit the small change;
and governments arranged a little war for when you got
older; and friends, relatives, even strangers wished you
many fine years on the muckheap, as they pursued their
blindfolded, arms-folded lives and politely helped
each other into the oven. And everybody promised you
your own place in the oven, your own meat hook,
your own hole in the head, own hole in the ground,
as they shut down their brains to the destruction
and stultifying boredom and once more decided
to keep their money on the big promise: the spirit
of this country rising out of the east like a great
red mouth—tearing and rending, devouring its children.

GENERAL MATTHEI DRIVES HOME
THROUGH SANTIAGO

The part where General Matthei leaves his office,
I don't know about. And when he gets home,
that I don't know about either. Or if he had
a hard day or an easy day or if his secretary
bent down in front of him so he could see her
large breasts or if he has a secretary or if she has breasts—
all this remains shrouded in mystery. Likewise,
when he got home, whether his four Dobermans
romped out to greet him or if he spent his evening
polishing his pistolas—this too is hidden from me.
But I know for certain it takes twelve men to help
General Matthei drive home; it takes five vehicles:
two motorcycles with sirens and three big gray cars.
Were they Mercedes? They were going too fast to tell.
As for why it is necessary for him to hurry home
so rapidly, this too is a mystery, except
that each day he requires twelve men, five vehicles
and most of the speed in Santiago. It has been said
his bowels were shot away in a duel and the poor general
must spend his life rushing from bathroom to bathroom.
It has been said that as general of the air force
he fears the earth as the wealthy fear the poor.
Or perhaps he is jealous of his wife or has bread
baking in the oven or is accustomed to watching
the American cartoons on the TV at seven-thirty.
But the other generals of the Junta also rush home
at 100 kilometers per hour down the crowded *avenidas*.
Surely they are not all jealous of their wives.
So again the curtain of mystery is lowered before us.
But yesterday as I was driving home and the general
was driving home and about a million other residents
of Santiago were also going home, I saw the small
humiliation of a middle-aged woman in a small red Fiat
who was neither beautiful, nor was she driving fast.

Maybe she was thinking about her dinner or maybe
her car radio was turned up and she was singing
to the music. In any case, she didn't hear the sirens.
The military policeman riding the first motorcycle
wore white leather gauntlets that nearly reached
his elbows, and when the red Fiat had the audacity
not to scramble for the curb, he swerved around it
and smashed his fist down hard on the red Fiat's hood.
For an instant, that was the loudest noise in Santiago.
Did the red Fiat leap several feet in the air?
I believe it did. Then it braked and swerved right and
dozens of other cars braked and swerved right and blew
their horns and in that moment the general was gone.
I wish I could say all this led to some small tragedy—
that the red Fiat smashed the cart of a man selling bread
or ran over a dog or the woman swallowed her teeth.
But this was a normal evening in late spring and the sky
was as blue as ever and the lowering sun had just begun
to redden the tips of the snowcapped Andes and in another
moment the tangled cars straightened themselves out
and the woman in the red Fiat simply drove home.
When she arrived, maybe she told her husband about
the general and maybe he went out and stared at the Fiat
but saw nothing but a smear in the dust on the red hood.
But maybe he looked at it and the rest of his family
looked at it and maybe he mentioned it to some friends
and they looked at it too. And someday when General Matthei
is shot and dragged by his heels through the streets,
this man will think of his red Fiat and suck his teeth
and, in a way that is typical of the people of Santiago,
he will half roll and half shrug one of his shoulders
as if letting a heavy strap at last slide from it.

DANCING IN VACATIONLAND

The people in the houses behind Searsport are dancing:
the people in tin and tar-paper mobile homes, people
in plywood shacks surrounded by junked cars and tires,
broken furniture, hungry geese and chickens, bored
hunting dogs. In ones and twos, they open their doors,
weaving and bobbing out to the road: men in gray
work clothes, women in baggy print dresses; the people
who process chickens, stick fingers down chicken throats
as the chickens come dangling down the line, tearing
out windpipes, tearing out guts; the men and women
who pick meat out of crab bodies, arrange sardines
in little cans; men who work the docks in all weather,
who try to run lobster boats throughout the winter.
These people are now dancing from their houses of
wreckage where they scream at each other and raise
ignorant children and hang on to each other at night.
In threes and fours, they dance toward Searsport and
Route 1. Then, reaching town, they form a single line
dancing with their arms on their neighbors' shoulders,
dancing in one long row between the shiny antique shops
and fat realtors: one foot up, one foot down, step
to the right, step to the left—lining the highway
which is crowded with tourists from the south
trying to soak up picturesque views of the ocean.
But this morning all they can see are people dancing,
these bloated potato-fed people dancing, these people
who live by collecting returnable bottles, by picking
over the trash at the dump, by trading their bodies
their wits, their health for a few dollars
and a shack behind Searsport. This morning, because
it is warm and sunny and because they just can't
stand it anymore, they decided to start dancing:
one foot up, one foot down. And the tourists from New York
stop their cars and the tourists from Massachusetts

take pictures and the tourists from Connecticut
feed candy to the little ones, until at last the realtors
and tour-guide directors and lobster-shack owners,
until at last the alternative-life-style farmers,
gift-shop operators, local chamber of commerce,
town police, state police and sheriff's department
all band together and a spokesperson apologizes
to the tourists from the south and begs them
to take no more pictures; and they try to make
the people stop dancing, but the people won't listen
and keep right on dancing—one foot up, one foot down—
so they push them back off Route 1, push them back
to the little roads behind Searsport, push them back
into the tin and tar-paper mobile homes, the plywood
shacks surrounded by junked cars, but through the windows
they can still be seen dancing, dancing into the night
in their little paper houses, until at last they lie down
and hold on to each other, hang on to each other
as if afraid of sinking into the earth, afraid the whole
vacationland world might stop spinning beneath them.

for Kevin Boyle

Two men walk along the edge of a country road.
One is joking and talking about girls, describing
the abrupt curve from waist to buttocks and how
it sometimes seems the whole world lives there.
As he talks, he idly tosses rocks into the field
on his right, a field of purple clover spotted
with yellow flowers. The rocks clip the flowers or
green leaves, then disappear into the darkness beneath.
It is a cloudless afternoon in midsummer
and in the distance a green locomotive drags
a string of red boxcars toward the horizon.

The other man has hardly eaten for two days.
He is silent and has almost made up his mind
that when they reach the shelter of the woods
half a mile distant, he will rob his companion,
whom he met only that morning. He has a knife
and intends only to show it, but if the other man
wants to fight, well, so much the worse for him.
And he imagines how the knife will slide up
under the ribs, how he'll drag the body off the road,
then escape over the field to the railway line.
So, while the one man talks about girls,
the other tries to steel himself and feel hatred
for his companion, tries to make him the focus
for all that has gone wrong in his life—
the loss of his job, desertion of his family.

Shortly, the man talking about girls begins
to think of his wife, whom he hasn't seen
for nearly a month. And partly he talks
to keep from thinking about her and partly
to keep her a teasing question in his mind.
Will she still love him? Has she found someone else?

He thinks of times they made love when he would
sit back on his haunches straddling her ankles
and see how her body was spread out beneath him;
and as he talks the memory of his wife naked
upon the bed fills his mind, while the rocks he
tosses into the field become the fears of betrayal
and desertion that one by one he pushes from him.

Days later the other man is arrested in the city
and as he awaits the slow unfolding of justice
he tells himself how foolish his companion
had been with his constant talk about girls
and how he deserved all that had happened.
He has no sense of himself as a fragment.
He has no sense of how he and his dead companion
made up one man. Add a third and he's still
one man; add a fourth, likewise. But by himself,
he's a fragment of wall, part of a broken pot;
he's like the quivering rodent under its
protection of leaves, terrified when the chance
rock crashes through its green ceiling, victim
of a world that is endlessly random and violent.

WIND CHIMES

Begin with a Victorian cottage in a Rhode Island
resort town—a two-story house of yellow shingles
a block from the ocean with a roof like a Chinese
pagoda and a screened-in porch on three sides.
A wooden croquet set lies scattered on the lawn
which is surrounded by a chest-high privet hedge.
Hanging from the porch ceiling, a wind chimes
with eight glass bars swings gently in a breeze
smelling of salt and fried food from hot-dog stands
along the beach. In the middle of the living room,
a boy lies on his stomach reading a Batman comic.
Around him are wicker chairs with white cushions.
The boy's knees are bent and the soles of his tattered
gym shoes point toward the ceiling. As he reads,
he slowly bumps his heels together as if in time
to the sound of the surf he hears in the distance.
A collie dog lies panting at the foot of the stairs,
while in a bedroom at the top of the stairs
a man lies naked on white sheets smoking a cigarette.
His wife, also naked, sleeps with her head on his chest.
As he smokes, the man carelessly strokes her back and
stares up at the lines and angles of the white ceiling
until it seems he's looking down from some high place,
a plane or hilltop. From where he lies, he can just see
the roofs of other houses and he imagines his neighbors
drowsing their way through the August afternoon.
White curtains sway in the breeze from the open window,
while the smoke from his cigarette seems to turn blue
as it rises through bars of sunlight to the ceiling.
From nearby, the man hears the sound of people
playing tennis—an occasional shout and the plonk
of the ball against the webbing of the racket;
from the porch, he hears the tinkling of wind chimes
like a miniature orchestra forever warming up.
▪ ▪ ▪

Years later the same man is lying fully clothed
on his bed in a city hotel. It is evening and
the only light comes from the street and a blinking
red sign outside his window. He's waiting for a friend
and soon they will go out to dinner, but as he waits
he watches the shadows on the ceiling and either that
reminds him of the wind chimes or perhaps
it is some combination of sounds from the street.
His son is grown up; his wife has remarried.
He himself has a new wife in another city
and he's away from home only because of his work
in which he thinks himself happy and successful.
But for a moment, he clearly hears the wind chimes,
sees the swaying curtains in that summer bedroom,
even feels the faint pressure of his ex-wife's
sleeping head upon his chest. But then
it slips by and in its place he has an awareness
of all the complicated turnings of his life,
and he wonders if what he had seen as progress
was only a scrambling after circumstance, like a boy
trying to scramble into the back of a moving truck;
and while he doesn't regret his life, he grieves
for all that was lost, all that he had to let go.
He thinks of that ocean house and wishes he were back
in his former life or that one could take one moment
and remain inside it like an egg inside its shell,
instead of constantly being hurried into the future
by good luck or bad. Again he hears the wind chimes,
even sees them hanging in the dark with their
eight glass bars and red Oriental designs, but then
they begin to get smaller as if quickly receding,
until they are no more than a speck of bright light
which at last blinks out as his friend starts hammering
at the door and his whole busy life rushes forward.

BLEEDER

By now I bet he's dead which suits me fine,
but twenty-five years ago when we were both
fifteen and he was a camper and I counselor
in a straitlaced Pennsylvania summer camp
for crippled and retarded kids, I'd watch

him sit all day by himself on a hill. No trees
or sharp stones: he wasn't safe to be around.
The slightest bruise and all his blood would simply
drain away. It drove us crazy—first
to protect him, then to see it happen. I

would hang around him, picturing a knife
or pointed stick, wondering how small a cut
you'd have to make, then see the expectant face
of another boy watching me, and we each knew
how much the other would like to see him bleed.

He made us want to hurt him so much we hurt
ourselves instead: sliced fingers in craft class,
busted noses in baseball, then joined at last
into mass wrestling matches beneath his hill,
a tangle of crutches and braces, hammering at

each other to keep from harming him. I'd look up
from slamming a kid in the gut and see him watching
with the empty blue eyes of children in sentimental
paintings, and hope to see him frown or grin,
but there was nothing: as if he had already died.

Then, after a week, they sent him home. Too much
responsibility, the director said.
Hell, I bet the kid had skin like leather.
Even so, I'd lie in bed at night and think
of busting into his room with a sharp stick, lash

• • •

and break the space around his rose-petal flesh,
while campers in bunks around me tossed and dreamt
of poking and bashing the bleeder until he
was left as flat as a punctured water balloon,
which is why the director sent him home. For what

is virtue but the lack of strong temptation;
better to leave us with our lie of being good.
Did he know this? Sitting on his private hill,
watching us smash each other with crutches and canes,
was this his pleasure: to make us cringe beneath

our wish to do him damage? But then who cared?
We were the living children, he the ghost
and what he gave us was a sense of being bad
together. He took us from our private spite
and offered our bullying a common cause:

which is why we missed him, even though we wished
him harm. When he left, we lost our shared meanness
and each of us was left to snarl his way
into a separate future, eager to discover
some new loser to link us in frailty again.

FUNNY

These guys, it's hard to believe these guys.
They're stuck in a halfway house for half-crazy vets
at the top of the hill and they stroll through town
with their hands in their pockets or waving at cars.

Or you see them in bars eating an ice cream cone
or maybe drinking beer, although with all that
medication you'd think they couldn't drink, but
what the heck they've probably got lobotomies. Anyway

they'll sit in a bar like Curly, Moe and Shemp
grinning and staring at the girls, I mean, any
girls or sometimes they'll just focus on a blank
spot on the wall or a flickering Budweiser sign.

One time one of them crept up behind the city
council president who was sipping a martini
and he's got orange hair like a dandelion clock
and this crazy vet just ruffled it like you might

rub down a watermelon or feel a tit. The guy from
the council swore he'd never seen the vet before,
although you wonder how he ever missed him, and he
would have decked him if the vet hadn't left so quick.

They all wear funny hats to either warm their brains
or keep their heads from popping off, you don't know which.
And they look like teenagers somehow, although they're
pushing fifty. One of them keeps his graying hair

in a perfect duck's ass haircut, wears a jacket with
padded shoulders and makes wolf whistles at girls.
I keep picturing him in Korea on Hill 366
like in that movie with Gregory Peck, and the Chinese

keep shelling them all day and night and each shell
clicks his life another notch toward Belfast, Maine.
And this guy, he's probably from Nebraska or someplace
and he quit high school in 1951 and took a job

in a garage so he can work on his car, a 1948
purple Merc with a chopped top so the windshield's
only six inches high and double chrome pipes and
huge chrome bumpers, and I think of this guy

trying to peer into that chrome, because in his head
it's still 1951 even though he's sitting in the Belfast
Cafe with an ice cream cone, and he's searching
for his face in the chrome, but it's distorted

like in a trick mirror, and he can't see it's him,
can't see it's his old motorcycle cap, his DA haircut,
his scarred forehead, his wandering and witless
fifty-year-old eyes. Now that's what I call funny.

for Michael Hurley

Drill holes in small rocks, then press your lips
to each hole and blow. One by one the rocks
get bigger, edges sharper. This is what I've
got in my stomach that the dopes call anger.
Just writing it makes me want to smack my face,
break this pen. The same dopes will all tell you
a thing of beauty is a joy forever, well I guess
that lets me out. Let me explain what I mean:
not long ago in Spain I stood on a cliff above
the city of Jaén, above the gray of its cathedral,
the pink stone high-rises thrown up for workers.
It'd been raining all morning and gray sky reached out
hundreds of miles over the abused red clay land
where every fifteen feet grew another olive tree:
millions of trees with twisted dark trunks and
wet leaves pointing in millions of directions
like nervousness or love in a flutter. My anger
was with me then in the rain and I wanted to
chip and chisel it free from my body, leave it
like a heavy stone at the bottom of deep water.
I wanted to drift out above that olive-covered land
until my body broke apart like clouds or spring rain.
Two feet stuck in angry dirt is no way to do a life.
Far below me houses hunkered down like warts on a hand,
as narrow streets twisted and intersected: turning,
turning back on themselves, always back on themselves.

THIS LIFE

> "Maestro, chi son qulle genti che l'aura nera si gastiga?"
> —*Canto V,* The Inferno

Blue sky to the south, clouds to the north,
racing tatters of cloud in between—although
here only the first flakes have begun to fall,
in the distance the mountains are tugging on
their winter caps. Outside, a spiral of snow
whirls between window and forest's edge
like a man fighting his way out of a sheet.
Inside, this is a college class on translation.
The teacher recites the line: " 'I love
this poor earth because I know no other.'
Is it earth or country? What difference
does this make?"
                  Once more I think of you
six thousand miles south in your poor country,
and again I count all the possible reasons
why I haven't heard from you—bad mail,
bad politics, bad love. I think of how Dante
condemned his lovers to an existence of wind
and try to imagine us brought together
in the frantic white spiral that rushes between
the window and winter trees. To be so joined to you—
the thought brings my heart to my throat.
But without you—that's me out there alone.
Blue sky to the south, clouds to the north—
in another hour when this class is over
and the wall of cloud has reached the horizon,
the spiral of snow will have vanished: lost
in that falling white blanket, this life,
which as we return to our separate rooms
we will say is so impossible to walk through.

WHERE WE ARE

After Bede

A man tears a chunk of bread off the brown loaf,
then wipes the gravy from his plate. Around him
at the long table, friends fill their mouths
with duck and roast pork, fill their cups from
pitchers of wine. Hearing a high twittering, the man

looks to see a bird—black with a white patch
beneath its beak—flying the length of the hall,
having flown in by a window over the door. As straight
as a taut string, the bird flies beneath the roofbeams,
as firelight flings its shadow against the ceiling.

The man pauses—one hand holds the bread, the other
rests upon the table—and watches the bird, perhaps
a swift, fly toward the window at the far end of the room.
He begins to point it out to his friends, but one is
telling hunting stories, as another describes the best way

to butcher a pig. The man shoves the bread in his mouth,
then slaps his hand down hard on the thigh of the woman
seated beside him, squeezes his fingers to feel the firm
muscles and tendons beneath the fabric of her dress.
A huge dog snores on the stone hearth by the fire.

From the window comes the clicking of pine needles
blown against it by an October wind. A half moon
hurries along behind scattered clouds, while the forest
of black spruce and bare maple and birch surrounds
the long hall the way a single rock can be surrounded

by a river. This is where we are in history—to think
the table will remain full; to think the forest will
remain where we have pushed it; to think our bubble of
good fortune will save us from the night—a bird flies in
from the dark, flits across a lighted hall and disappears.

BLACK DOG, RED DOG

The boy waits on the top step, his hand on the door
to the screen porch. A green bike lies in the grass,
saddlebags stuffed with folded newspapers. The street
is lined with maples in full green of summer, white houses
set back from the road. The man whom the boy has come
to collect from shuffles onto the porch. As is his custom,
he wears a gray dress with flowers. Long gray hair
covers his shoulders, catches in a week's growth of beard.
The boy opens the door and glancing down he sees yellow
streaks of urine running down the man's legs, snaking
into the gray socks and loafers. For a year, the boy
has delivered the man's papers, mowed and raked his lawn.
He's even been inside the house which stinks of excrement
and garbage, with forgotten bags of groceries on tables:
rotten fruit, moldy bread, packages of unopened hamburger.
He would wait in the hall as the man counted out pennies
from a paper bag, adding five extra out of kindness.
The boy thinks of when the man's mother was alive.
He would sneak up to the house when the music began
and watch the man and his mother dance cheek to cheek
around the kitchen, slowly, hesitantly, as if each
thought the other could break as easily as a china plate.
The mother had been dead a week when a neighbor found her
and even then her son wouldn't let her go. The boy sat
on the curb watching the man hurl his fat body against
the immaculate state troopers who tried not to touch him
but only keep him from where men from the funeral home
carried out his mother wrapped in red blankets, smelling
like hamburger left for weeks on the umbrella stand.

Today as the boy waits on the top step watching the urine
trickle into the man's socks, he raises his head to see
the pale blue eyes fixed upon him with their wrinkles and
bags and zigzagging red lines. As he stares into them,
he begins to believe he is staring out of those eyes,

looking down at a thin blond boy on his front steps.
Then he lifts his head and still through the man's eyes
he sees the softness of late afternoon light on the street
where the man has spent his entire life, sees the green
of summer, white Victorian houses as through a white fog
so they shimmer and flicker before him. Looking past
the houses, past the first fields, he sees the reddening
sky of sunset, sees the land rushing west as if it wanted
to smash itself as completely as a cup thrown to the floor,
violently pursuing the sky with great spirals of red wind.

Abruptly the boy steps back. When he looks again into
the man's eyes, they appear bottomless and sad; and he
wants to touch his arm, say he's sorry about his mother,
sorry he's crazy, sorry he lets urine run down his leg
and wears a dress. Instead, he gives him his paper
and leaves. As he raises his bike, he looks out toward
red sky and darkening earth, and they seem poised
like two animals that have always hated each other,
each fiercely wanting to tear out the other's throat:
black dog, red dog—now more despairing, more resolved.

FRENCHIE

I was eating a chicken sandwich with mayonnaise
and reading about Russia when Frenchie stumbled
into the restaurant for a free cup of coffee.
He was drunk, but not too drunk to speak. Around me
blue-haired ladies nibbled Sunday dinners along with
other respectable types: bank clerk and plumber.
When he saw me, Frenchie asked how I was doing,
even though he has disliked me ever since I
kept him from hitting an old man with his crutch.
Frenchie needs a crutch because of the night he
dared the cop in the cruiser to drive over his foot.

Frenchie stood swaying at the front of the restaurant,
glaring at the blue-haired ladies who tried not to notice.
His face looks like a track team once sprinted across it.
In my book, the wife of the Russian poet was saying:
What will our grandchildren make of it if we all
leave the scene in silence? It was then Frenchie
decided to throw his cup to the floor and announce
he was going to die. Fragments of cup scattered around
my seat. Frenchie shouted: I'm sick and going to die and
no one cares! We all ate very quietly, as if listening
to the pop-pop of our taste buds self-destructing.

The waitress touched his arm. Oh, Frenchie, she said;
as if he wouldn't die; as if we would, but he wouldn't.
Don't give me that, he said. He was crying now. We each
pretended not to listen and I stared hard at my book,
but I thought we all had begun to imagine our own last
moments, as if Frenchie had put us in little theaters and
there on a stage the curtains were being noisily raised
and the elderly ladies, bank clerk, plumber, waitress
and myself—we all saw our funerals enacted before us: one

with a son come from Dallas, another with a sad Irish setter:
heaps of flowers, buckets of tears and an organ playing Bach.

But it wasn't so funny, because here we were on a Sunday
afternoon and I was concentrating on my chicken sandwich
and book where the woman was saying: What we wouldn't
have given for ordinary heartbreaks. And all of us
were trying to consume our small pleasures or at least
diversions, and I bet some of these ladies think too much
about death anyway, and here's Frenchie shouting I'm going
to die which takes the joy out of the meatloaf and mashed
potatoes. As for Frenchie, he's pure spite. I've seen him
hit little kids and he stands outside of bars making faces
at people through the glass and giving them the finger,

and just because the waitress was kind enough to offer him
a free cup of coffee he decided to remind us of the death
lurking in our future. So when he shouted that he's going
to die, I wanted to say: Sure, Frenchie, and can you do it
in the next few minutes? Let me help you find a truck,
walk you out to the end of the dock. Hey, I know a man
who's got a rabid dog. But maybe I was supposed to be
nice to him, take him home to meet my wife and kid,
let my wife cook him up some beans and franks, let him
fool around with my kid, wear my shirts and sweaters,
let him pet the cat. Hell, he'd probably eat the cat.

So none of that took place. Instead, he stood there
shouting and his clothes were torn and he had vomit
on his shirt, and sure he would have liked someone
to give him ten bucks or a new life, but what he mostly
wanted was to grab us by our stomachs, our Sunday
dinners, yank us from our self-complacency and turn us
into witnesses, even though I had no wish to be a witness.

He wanted to make us take notice and say: Yes, you're
going to die, we're all going to die and that's too bad
and that's what sticks us in the same lousy boat
and no book or chicken sandwich will make it go away.

Maybe we should have stood up, confessed our mortality,
then crossed the street to the hardware that's open each
Sunday afternoon or wandered up to Barbara's Lunch or
the McDonald's out on the state highway. Maybe we ought
to have told everyone we met we were going to die and they
were going to die, until half the town is wandering around
tapping the other half on the shoulder, saying, Hey,
guess what? Then shake their hands and kiss them good-bye.
Maybe that would have been best, because in the restaurant
we all played dumb and nobody did a damn thing except
the waitress who said: Come on, Frenchie, you better go now.

As for me, I finished my sandwich, closed my book, pushed
past Frenchie and left, hoping to miss the tantrums,
the cops, the broken glass. But in the next few months,
I kept noticing Frenchie around town and he still
hadn't died, although twice I saw him being tossed
into the back of a cop car. Then this morning I see him
again as I'm driving through town, and it's a bright
blue morning at the beginning of March, and Frenchie
and a buddy are sunning themselves out in front of
the U-Ota-Bowl Alleys, and they're passing a bottle,
slapping their knees and having a high old time.

From this I guess Frenchie has forgotten he is
going to die, and I want to hang a U-turn, pull up
in front with my brand-new unpaid-for Volkswagen,
get out wearing my fashionable corduroys, down jacket
and expensive boots. Then I want to grab Frenchie

by the ears, kiss him smack on his vomit mouth,
sit down, drink a little Old Duke Red, tell a few
spiteful jokes, slap my knee and remind him that I'm
his witness, because even though he has forgotten
he is going to die, I haven't and what's more I'm
going to die too, as is his buddy, but what the hell.

In fact, maybe I should give him the car and down jacket,
not from guilt or that I've had better luck, but because
we're both going down the same slide. But who am I kidding?
I neither stopped my car nor waved, but drove straight to
my office with its books, papers, and other shields against
the darkness, and after wasting time and making coffee and
staring out the window, I at last saw no hope for it and I
wrote down these words not because I saw myself in his eyes,
but from nothing more complicated than embarrassment.
The only way out of this life is to take him with me:
the left hand can't pretend it doesn't know the right.

for Jay Davis

The woman who kicked out the back window
of the police cruiser sits chain-smoking and
drinking at a table by the dance floor.
Watching from a barstool, you doubt she
weighs over a hundred pounds. She is gaunt,
bony and resembles a fierce pygmy
warrior. One time she ripped off her clothes
in the parking lot, defied police to touch her.
Another time she pursued a patrolman
down the street, then kicked him in the balls.
Maybe she's twenty. Here in the bar she
seems jittery, can't hold her liquor, people
tell you, which is probably true, but you also
respect someone who knows she has nothing
to lose. You too have nothing to lose but spend
much of your time telling yourself you do.
In fact, it seems the point of society is to
make people think they have something to lose
until a man goes through life as nervously
as if he were carrying a teetery
stack of plates up a dark flight of stairs.

When the woman who kicked out the window
of the cop car dances, she shrugs her shoulders
and stamps her feet very fast as if she
weren't dancing but stamping on a multitude
of grievances. Mostly she dances by herself
because few men will ask her. You nearly
ask her, then change your mind, telling yourself
you are shy; but really you fear that you too
are something she can easily let go,
fear she'll see through your equivocations,
realize you think you have something to lose
and simply guffaw. Why dance with her at all?

Perhaps you think she might instruct you how
to shove aside the trappings of your life,
because in her life nothing's there for keeps,
or so it seems, and you wish you had that
freedom from the things you own, but you don't
so at last you give it up and go home.
It's a clear spring night. In the parking lot,
two cops lean against their cruiser, staring
at the sky and idly waiting for trouble.

Are these the bad guys? Walking to your car,
you think of the fabric of value that surrounds you
as like the night itself, as if you could
poke your finger through it, as if the spots
of light you call stars were the places where
the great doubters of history had jabbed their thumbs.
The younger cop nods hello. You wonder
if they are waiting for the fierce woman
and if you should protect her, remove your
clothes and shout: Take me, take me. But you're not
the one they want in jail. You may have doubts,
but none to break the law for. As you drive home
beside the ocean, the moonpath follows you
on the water like a long finger of light.
Blame me, you say, go ahead, blame me.
Tomorrow you'll buy something you think you'll need,
ditto the next day, ditto the day after that.
Once home, you close and lock yourself inside,
as if you were both guard and prisoner—
prisoner with a question mark in your future
and no days off for your best behavior.

KENTUCKY DERBY DAY, BELFAST, MAINE

When I was twelve, I happened to guess the winning horse
of the Kentucky Derby. It was on the sixth-grade
field trip to the Henry Ford Museum where we learned
that plain common sense is the key to the moral dominance
of the United States. The man on the car radio discussed
the horses and when he came to the name Dark Star, I said,
That's the horse for me. I mean, it seemed clear that any
horse named Dark Star *had* to win; and when Dark Star won,
I said, Sure—because in sixth grade life was like that.
My teacher said, Hey, you could have won a bundle.
I thought, What could be more simple? From that event
I date my readiness to be stupid about racehorses.

So on this May 2nd twenty-eight years later I shut down
my typewriter at five o'clock and hurry across to
Barbara's Lunch to watch the 107th running of the Derby.
It's been a lousy day and instead of writing or reading or
cleaning up my desk, I keep brooding that my marriage
is breaking apart, that my life seems aimed at a ditch,
is clearly out of control, and in the ornate bar mirror
I see my hair standing up in attitudes of bewilderment.
The restaurant is closed, TV dark and bar empty except for
the bartender, who's barely twenty and just learning to mix
cocktails, and a table of five people from the chicken plant
who I bet have been drinking beer and shots since breakfast.

Two of them are fast fat girls in tight shorts and loose
blouses and one wears a dog collar. Then there's a boy
as thin as a razor who has snipped off the sleeves of
his jean jacket and has homemade tattoos on his biceps
and bare shoulders. Another is a chain-smoking old man
destined, I'm sure, to die of cancer. And lastly
there is Leo, who resembles an aging country-western
singer, with a chin like a brick and thinning brown hair

swept back to look like Johnny Cash. The girl with
the dog collar strokes Leo's hand and tells the boy:
We love each other; we fight, but we love each other.
The boy nods. Although no Apollo, he knows about love.

But this is Derby Day: twenty-one eager horses
and I'm told Tap Shoes is the horse to beat so I
call over to the bartender and say, Hey, turn on the TV
and let's watch the Derby. He says, What's the Derby?
And I say, The Kentucky Derby. And he says, I never
heard of it. But he's a nice kid so he flicks on the TV
and there's Churchill Downs and thousands of flowers and
happy fans. Jesus, says the kid, look at all those people!
It's the Derby, I say: See, there's Muhammad Ali.
Who's that? says the kid. You know, I say, the great boxer.
Hey, says the kid, those horses going to pull little carts?
Not today, I say. Too bad, says the kid, I like the carts.

On the TV the announcer is predicting how the race
will be run and famous people are asked their opinions.
I wait for a twinkle in my brain but nothing happens. Still
it's all so exciting I want to talk to someone about it—
say how making a bet is like falling in love or that
the horses and jockeys look like centaurs before the rape
of whoever—but the bartender is learning to make a Pink Lady,
while the five chicken processors are deep in their sadness.
The girl with the collar puts her hand on the boy's shoulder
and says, He needs me, Joey, I don't care if he hits me,
he wouldn't hit me if he didn't need to do it. And Leo says,
Hey, I'm no good. She thinks I'm good but I'm a pig.

The light from the door throws their shadows on the wall.
I think how defeated their lives are and wonder why
the girl wears a dog collar and what Leo must do
to mistreat her, if the old man will really die of cancer

162

and why the boy sticks holes in his arms to make dumb
tattoos with the name Jesse and little stars and crosses,
how he will die with that sentimental doodling still
on his body, having spent his life as a poor man's
advertisement for unrequited love. In no time I start
thinking of my own life with its insoluble problems—
how I can't afford health insurance and my parents
constantly fret and that my marriage is falling apart.

But on the TV they're getting ready for the run for
the roses—one hundred and forty thousand happy fans.
Maybe Bold Ego, I tell myself. Maybe Cure the Blues
or Proud Appeal. Maybe Top Avenger or Mythical Ruler.
What noble names. They all deserve to win. The bartender
looks up from his little red guide. I like gray horses best,
he says, it makes them look sad. Now they're in the gate.
The TV's by the jukebox and the flashing lights become all
the flowers at Churchill Downs. Then the bell and they're off!
Right away the horses string out rounding the first turn as
the favorites take an early lead. But oh-oh here come the girl
with the dog collar with about five bucks for the jukebox.

Hold up, I tell her, this is a big race and it's almost over.
She's indifferent but polite so she waits. What's your horse?
she asks. Maybe Bold Ego, I say, unable to see him. I love
those country songs, says the girl. She stands beside me
and when I look down, I find I can look down her blouse.
But on the TV terrible things are happening: all the heroic
names are falling behind and coming up fast at the finish
is Pleasant Colony, while the number two horse, Woodchopper,
pays over twenty dollars and I'll bet they never announced
his name, because I spent half the damn winter chopping wood
and if I'd put a thousand on Woodchopper or even a hundred,
then right now I'd be winging my way south to better times.
▪ ▪ ▪

Troy has fallen, I tell the girl, play those country songs.
She puts a hand on my arm. It's a crazy world, she says.
And I say, What's a smart girl like you doing here
in Barbara's Lunch? Why, she says, we're just waiting
for Big John to get us out of here. Aren't we all, I say.
The girl feeds her five bucks into the slot and goes back
to Leo, drapes herself over his shoulder as the jukebox
begins to pound out "Take These Chains from My Heart,"
which drowns out the TV where Pleasant Colony and jockey
Jorge Velasquez and trainer John Campo and the owner
Thomas Mellon Evans accept the quarter-of-a-million-
dollar purse and their corner on the world's happiness.

As I watch the horseshoe of roses being lowered onto
Pleasant Colony's neck, I think of my life and wonder
how to cope with my marriage coming down to certain divorce
and a son who will be the subject of long-distance calls
and for whom I'll be an occasional visitor. Is he taller?
I will ask. Is he doing well in school? And I will remember
kissing the soft part of his neck, the velvet indentation by
his collarbone, how I would nuzzle it and he would giggle.
On the TV the winners keep mouthing their thanks to the world
as the jukebox plays songs of infidelity and rejected love
and the girl with the dog collar keeps glancing at the door,
waiting for Big John who is a phenomenon I have no faith in.

But dammit all, I'm wrong. Just when I think it's a joke
in comes this big fellow and the girl jumps to her feet.
It's Big John, she says. And Big John looks foolish and grins.
He's a fat man in a red T-shirt that doesn't reach
his waist so the roll of fat looks like a white snake
wrapped round his belly. But everybody's perking up
and the girls twitch their shoulders. Come on, shouts
the one with the dog collar, Big John's got his Winnebago.

So we troop out to the street where the fog's rolling in and
parked at the curb is a golden Winnebago with a huge stereo,
soft chairs and all the beer you can drink. So what if you
don't know horses? So what if your life's shot to hell?

Hey, I shout, can your fat god in his fat machine fix my life?
Happy days ahead, calls the girl, hanging from the back step.
But before I can decide to act, Big John hits the gas.
The gutters of Belfast are filled with the white feathers
of chickens trucked daily to the processing plant, and as
Big John takes off feathers are swept up in his wake like
a taste of hot times. The Winnebago disappears into the fog,
like some wingèd Pegasus, I think, or Trojan Horse cruising
the coastline for holiday villages to pillage and burn.
In any case, it's gone and on the dead streets of Belfast
I find myself stuck without wonderful racehorse, joke
or sad life with which to divert myself by watching.

Where are the tricks to help me through the day? It's here
I must take my first step but I'm torn between Dark Star,
the Winnebago life or finding my way home where my wife tries
to push me from her heart because I've told her she must.
Think of the wedding pictures and everybody laughing.
Think of all the contemptible ways to say good-bye.
And unable to move a foot, I turn this way and that:
Dark Star, Dark Star, where are the winners I was promised?
But I'm not dumb; I know you only win when you bet real money
and play for keeps. Instead, I stand in the street as feathers
drift over my shoulders. Like Icarus? I ask myself, hopefully.
No, just another damn fool who won't make up his mind.

NIGHT SWIMMER

Lifting his arms, the man half swims,
half thrashes his way to the dark shore
where he shakes himself, then threads a path
between the rocks to the first trees
where his horse is tied. Behind him
he has left two dead children whom he
found sleeping on cool summer sheets.
He had swum to the island to kill them
and, having finished his work, he unties
his horse and leads it quietly to the road.
Meanwhile, the father, who imagines his two sons
asleep in bed, stands at the other end
of the island, looking out over the lake.
High to his left hangs a half moon,
while near it is the constellation Orion.
The father thinks how his friends far off
in his own country see the same sky,
the same constellations, and it strikes him
that the three stars of Orion's belt
hang over his country like a finger.
Once more he begins his old argument
that for too long he has hidden himself
from the life of his homeland, that he must
return and help put his country in order.
Glancing back at his house, he sees a light
in the attic which then moves down the stairs,
and he guesses that a servant has gone
to cover the children. It is a square
white house and through the French windows
of his study, he sees the gray cat sleeping
on the papers on his desk. The night is windy
and the moon glimmers on rough water.
From the mainland, he hears the faint
clatter of hoofbeats and he wonders

what kind of person would be riding
so late and so far from home. Again
he thinks of the road to his own country
so that his desire to return and his fear
of defeat sway back and forth as he
considers the dangers and chances of success,
until he decides at last that he must
give up his exile, that it's not too late.
He thinks that once joined with his friends
they will destroy their enemies whose
only strength lies in their separation.
He looks back at his house where he hears
people shouting and calling his name
and so completely is he wrapped up
in his thoughts of returning that it seems
the servants have guessed his intentions
and are dragging the trunks down from the attic.
Across the lawn one of the servants
runs toward him, an old man whose white hair
and nightshirt flutter in the wind.
Eagerly, the father hurries to greet him
and he doesn't notice how the servant
is crying, how his arms are outstretched.
Instead, he calls out they are leaving,
and in his mind is a confused memory
of cafés and wide boulevards, of sitting
with his friends on spring evenings, arguing
and feeling indignant about the world
in those days before his children were born
when he had only his own good name to lose.

DEAD BABY

(Helen Johnston, 1882–1968)

My great-aunt had a story she often repeated
when she was old and losing her memory
about driving out to take care of a sick baby.
She was a nurse and this was one of her first cases
so it must have been around the turn of the century.
The baby's mother lived in a big house on Leyden Hill.
It was winter and my aunt had to go in the sleigh.
She was a slender woman, not much over five feet,
and easily frightened of her world going out of control
and by what she called rough men. She never married.
The house was a square, three-story Victorian house
and when my aunt got there she discovered the baby
dead in its crib, and the mother—apparently alone
in the house—exhausted and hysterical. By then
it was dark, and my aunt sent the woman to bed,
saying she would sit with the dead child. Eventually,
my aunt fell asleep only to be waked late at night by
the bump and scrape of someone limping across the floor.
By the light of the candle, she saw a blind man
stumbling toward her and she leapt from her chair.
Here my aunt would often stop as if having reached
the conclusion. Then she would look uncertain
and ask if I had ever heard the story she had told
at the banquet honoring her fifty years of nursing;
at which point, she would begin the whole story again—
the news of the sick baby, the sleigh, the discovery
of its death, the blind man stumbling through the dark.
But each time she told it she would add new details,
so when the man approached with his arms outstretched
my aunt saw that both arms had been cut off at the wrist,
that he was feeling his way forward with the two stumps.
Then, in another version, she saw that around one stump
the man had wrapped a rosary of jet-black beads.
My aunt said she flattened herself against the wall,

believing the blind man was after her, but then
he continued past her and made his way to the crib,
where he bent over and cried, fumbling his arms
against the dead baby, trying to embrace it, and how
he was unable to lift it, how it kept falling back.
After an hour he stumbled away in the dark, still
crying and bumping together the ruins of his arms.
In the morning, my aunt learned the man was a brother
who had been wounded in the Civil War, or in another
retelling she said he had been hurt in a train accident,
but perhaps the accident had taken place during the war.
My aunt would sit in her small room in a home for
the elderly, a gray stone building with thick walls,
supposedly the oldest house in Martinsburg, and say how
she wanted to go home and how unfair it all was.
Piled on a tray in front of her were stacks of cards
from relatives, neighbors, friends and old co-workers,
and as she talked she constantly picked through them
as if rereading the script of her life, as if
without these reminders it would all slip away and
she would sit there blankly, like a darkened lamp.
So each day she read out the names, retold her stories
and complained she was well enough to go home,
which she never did because she died in that room,
in that home for the elderly which later went broke
and is now a high-priced restaurant for skiers
up from New York. And I try to think of those
immaculate skiers eating prime rib in the room
where my aunt fumbled with her memory and repeated
her stories, always returning to the story of the baby,
as if the baby signified the remnants of her life,
by then mostly forgotten, but which she was still

trying to reclaim and embrace, in the way the blind
veteran with his hands sliced off at the wrist
had again and again tried to lift the baby from its crib
only to fail and feel it slip and fall away.

CUIDADORES DE AUTOS

It seems like the world's most useless profession—
to guard and protect the already safe and secure,
to guide you out of your parking place as if
this were your first time behind the wheel; as if
without their help you would smash into one car,
then another or collapse and weep uncontrollably;
that without them to put your peso in the meter,
you would desperately fumble, accidentally fling it
down the grating of a sewer. There must be
a thousand of these men on the streets of Santiago
with their symbols of office—a dirty
orange rag and a gray cap. I even know one man
who is training his son in the profession:
a boy of about eight with a smaller cap and
smaller rag. The father complains how people
ignore him, force him to chase them all the way
to the stoplight for his *propina* which is why he
employs his little boy who is quick on his feet
and likes to run. But I remember one night
when we had dinner at a restaurant near the market.
We had not argued that day. You were happy
and your eyes crinkled at the corners in a way
that makes you even more beautiful. When we
left the restaurant, yours was the only car still
on the block, and nearby waited one of these men,
these caretakers of cars, but older than most
and with a gray cap that looked like something
had been chewing it. He followed us to the car and
with great ceremony directed you away from the curb
with his little orange rag, peered intently into
the dark for any trucks that might be traveling
fast with their lights off. The world was safe
and the innocent slept soundly in their beds.
You thanked him, gave him ten pesos and he

called you his little daughter which pleased
and embarrassed you. The moon was full that night
but the moon here is not the northern moon;
the face is another face. The right eye that
I have seen all my life is now the mouth,
and the mouth of the north is now the left eye—
a face with a high forehead, no chin to speak of,
a leering, stupid sort of face which presumes
to know, but knows nothing. As you slept,
I studied the freckles on your back until they
seemed part of a map—towns with no roads
between them. Here everything feels reversed.
The fig tree in the back yard was heavy with figs
and I kept hearing them fall: first a brief riffle
as one dropped through the leaves, then a plop
like a wet, wadded-up sock as it hit the tiles
of the patio where it would harden and spoil.
You lay dreaming of houses—solar houses and
earthquake-proof houses, a house on the beach
with sunlight flickering on the white walls,
filling the rooms like water. And where was I?
Sometimes I hear sirens during curfew, the high
squealing sirens of the motorcycles; and that night
there were gunshots and the sound of running.
A German newspaper claims that last month
twenty-one houses were raided in Santiago,
442 political arrests. We know nothing of it.
Later that night a jeep slammed on its brakes.
There was shouting, the sound of someone being beaten.
We hurried outside. A young man lay in the grass,
moaning and holding his head. He said he had been
at a party. There had been a girl. He wore new
expensive-looking yellow boots and pleaded with us
not to call the police. Soon we went back to bed.

Who will protect us from our protectors?
As I lay beside you I listened to the sound of
the man's boots walking slowly down the street,
becoming fainter until at last they were lost
and grew confused with the pounding of my heart.

The worn plush of the seat chafes your bare legs
as you shiver in the air-conditioned dark
watching a man embrace his wife at the edge
of their shadowy lawn. It is just past dusk
and behind them their house rises white and
symmetrical. Candles burn in each window,
while from the open door a blade of light jabs
down the gravel path to a fountain. In the doorway
wait two children dressed for sleep in white gowns.
The man touches his wife's cheek. Although
he must leave, he is frightened for her safety and
the safety of their children. At last he hurries
to where two horses stamp and whinny in harness.
Then, from your seat in the third row, you follow him
through battles and bloodshed and friends lost
until finally he returns home: rides up the lane
as dusk falls to discover all that remains of his house
is a single chimney rising from ashes and mounds of debris.
Where is his young wife? He stares out across
empty fields, the wreckage of stables and barns.
Where are the children who were the comfort of his life?

In a few minutes, you plunge into the brilliant light
of the afternoon sun. Across the street, you see your bike
propped against a wall with your dog waiting beside it.
The dog is so excited to see you she keeps leaping up,
licking your face, while you, still full of the movie,
full of its color and music and lives sacrificed to some
heroic purpose, try to tell her about this unutterable
sadness you feel on a Saturday afternoon in July 1950.
Bicycling home, you keep questioning what happened
to the children, what happened to their father standing
by the burned wreckage of his house, and you wish
there were someone to explain this problem to, someone

to help you understand this sense of bereavement and loss:
you, who are too young even to regret the passage of time.
Next year your favorite aunt will die, then your
grandparents, one by one, then even your cousins.
You sit on the seat of your green bike with balloon tires
and watch your dog waiting up the street: a Bayeux
tapestry dog, brindle with thin legs and a greyhound chest,
a dog now no more than a speck of ash in the Michigan dirt.
From a distance of thirty years, you see yourself paused
at the intersection: a thin blond boy in khaki shorts;
see yourself push off into that afternoon sunlight,
clumsily entering your future the way a child urged on
by its frightened nurse might stumble into a plowed field
in the dead of night: half running, half pulled along.
Behind them: gunshots, flame and the crack of burning wood.
Far ahead: a black line of winter trees.

Now, after thirty years, the trees have come closer.
Glancing around you, you discover you are alone;
raising your hands to your face and beard, you find
you are no longer young, while the only fires
are in the fleck of stars above you, the only face
is the crude outline of the moon's: distant, as any family
you might have had; cold, in a way you have come to expect.

BEAUTY

The father gets a bullet in the eye, killing him
instantly. His daughter raises an arm to say stop
and gets shot in the hand. He's a grocer from Baghdad
and at that time lots of Iraqis are moving to Detroit
to open small markets in the ghetto. In a month,
three have been murdered and since it is becoming
old news your editor says only to pick up a photo
unless you can find someone half decent to talk to.

Jammed into the living room are twenty men in black,
weeping, and thirty women wailing and pulling their hair—
something not prepared for by your Episcopal upbringing.
The grocer had already given the black junkie his money
and the junkie was already out the door when he fired,
for no apparent reason, the cops said. The other daughter,
who gives you the picture, has olive skin, great dark eyes
and is so beautiful you force yourself to stare only

at the passport photo in order not to offend her.
The photo shows a young man with a thin face cheerfully
expecting to make his fortune in the black ghetto.
As you listen to the girl, the wailing surrounds you
like bits of flying glass. It was a cousin who was shot
the week before, then a good friend two weeks before that.
Who can understand it? During the riots, he told people
to take what they needed, pay when they were able.

Although the girl has little to do with your story,
she is, in a sense, the entire story. She is young,
beautiful and her father has just been shot. As you
accept the picture, her mother grabs it, presses it
to her lips. The girl gently pries her mother's fingers
from the picture and returns it. Then the sister with

the wounded hand snatches the picture and you want to
unwrap the bandages, touch your fingers to the bullet hole.

Again the girl retrieves the picture, but before she
can give it back, a third woman in black grabs it,
begins kissing it and crushing it to her bosom. You think
of the unflappable photographers on the fourth floor
unfolding the picture and trying to erase the creases,
but when the picture appears in the paper it still bears
the wrinkles of the fat woman's heart, and you feel caught
between the picture grabbing which is comic and the wailing

which is like an animal gnawing your stomach. The girl
touches your arm, asks if anything is wrong, and you say,
no, you only want to get out of there; and once back
at the paper you tell your editor of this room with fifty
screaming people, how they kept snatching the picture.
So he tells you about a kid getting drowned when he was
a reporter, but that's not the point, nor is the screaming,
nor the fact that none of this will appear in a news story

about an Iraqi grocer shot by a black drug addict,
and see, here is his picture as he looked when he first
came to our country eight years ago, so glad to get
out of Baghdad. What could be worse than Baghdad?
The point is in the sixteen-year-old daughter giving back
the picture, asking you to put it in your pocket, then
touching your arm, asking if you are all right and
would you like a glass of water? The point is she hardly

belongs to that room or any reality found in newspapers,
that she's one of the few reasons you get up in the morning,
pursue your life all day and why you soon quit the paper

to find her: beautiful Iraqi girl last seen surrounded by
wailing for the death of her father. For Christ's sake,
those fools at the paper thought you wanted to fuck her,
as if that's all you can do with something beautiful,
as if that's what it means to govern your life by it.

FROM CEMETERY NIGHTS
(1987)

Sweet dreams, sweet memories, sweet taste of earth:
here's how the dead pretend they're still alive—
one drags up a chair, a lamp, unwraps
the newspaper from somebody's garbage,
then sits holding the paper up to his face.
No matter if the lamp is busted and his eyes
have fallen out. Or some of the others
group together in front of the TV, chuckling
and slapping what's left of their knees.
No matter if the screen is dark. Four more
sit at a table with glasses and plates,
lift forks to their mouths and chew. No matter
if their plates are empty and they chew only air.
Two of the dead roll on the ground,
banging and rubbing their bodies together
as if in love or frenzy. No matter if their skin
breaks off, that their genitals are just a memory.

The head cemetery rat calls in all the city rats,
who pay him what rats find valuable—
the wing of a pigeon or ear of a dog.
The rats perch on tombstones and the cheap
statues of angels and, oh, they hold their bellies
and laugh, laugh until their guts half break;
while the stars give off the same cold light
that all these dead once planned their lives by,
and in someone's yard a dog barks and barks
just to see if some animal as dumb as he is
will wake from sleep and perhaps bark back.

THE GARDENER

After the first astronauts reached heaven
the only god discovered in residence
retired to a little brick cottage
in the vicinity of Venus. He was not
unduly surprised. He had seen it coming
since Luther. Besides, what with the imminence
of nuclear war, his job was nearly over.
As soon as the fantastic had become
a commonplace, bus tours were organized,
and once or twice a day the old fellow
would be trotted out from his reading of Dante
and asked to do a few tricks—lightning bolts,
water sprouting from a rock, blood from a turnip.
A few of the remaining cherubim
would fly in figure eights and afterward
sell apples from the famous orchard.
In the evening, the retired god would sometimes
receive a visit from his old friend the Devil.
They would smoke their pipes before the fire.
The Devil would stroke his whiskers and cover
his paws with his long furry tail. The mistake,
he was fond of saying, was to make them in
your image instead of mine. Possibly, said
the ex-deity. He hated arguing. The mistake,
he had often thought, was to experiment
with animal life in the first place when
his particular talent was as a gardener.
How pleasant Eden had been in those early days
with its neat rows of cabbages and beets,
flowering quince, a hundred varieties of rose.
But of course he had needed insects, and then
he made the birds, the red ones which he loved;
later came his experiments with smaller mammals—
squirrels and moles, a rabbit or two. When

the temptation had struck him to make something
really big, he had first conceived of it
as a kind of scarecrow to stand in the middle
of the garden and frighten off predators. What
voice had he listened to that convinced him
to give the creature his own face? No voice
but his own. It had amused him to make
a kind of living mirror, a little homunculus
that could learn a few of his lesser tricks.
And he had imagined sitting in the evening
with his friend the Devil watching the small
human creatures frolic in the grass. They would
be like children, good-natured and always singing.
When had he realized his mistake? Perhaps
when he smiled down at the first and it
didn't smile back; when he reached down to help
it to its feet and it shrugged his hand aside.
Standing up, it hadn't walked on the paths marked
with white stones but on the flowers themselves.
It's lonely, God had said. So he made it a mate,
then watched them feed on each other's bodies,
bicker and fight and trample through his garden,
dissatisfied with everything and wanting to escape.
Naturally, he hadn't objected. Kicked out,
kicked out, who had spread such lies? Shaking
and banging the bars of the great gate, they had
begged him for the chance to make it on their own.

TOMATOES

A woman travels to Brazil for plastic
surgery and a face-lift. She is sixty
and has the usual desire to stay pretty.
Once she is healed, she takes her new face
out on the streets of Rio. A young man
with a gun wants her money. Bang, she's dead.
The body is shipped back to New York,
but in the morgue there is a mix-up. The son
is sent for. He is told that his mother
is one of these ten different women.
Each has been shot. Such is modern life.
He studies them all but can't find her.
With her new face, she has become a stranger.
Maybe it's this one, maybe it's that one.
He looks at their breasts. Which ones nursed him?
He presses their hands to his cheek.
Which ones consoled him? He even tries
climbing into their laps to see which
feels most familiar but the coroner stops him.
Well, says the coroner, which is your mother?
They all are, says the young man, let me
take them as a package. The coroner hesitates,
then agrees. Actually, it solved a lot of problems.
The young man has the ten women shipped home,
then cremates them all together. You've seen
how some people have a little urn on the mantel?
This man has a huge silver garbage can.
In the spring, he drags the garbage can
out to the garden and begins working the teeth,
the ash, the bits of bone into the soil.
Then he plants tomatoes. His mother loved tomatoes.
They grow straight from seed, so fast and big
that the young man is amazed. He takes the first
ten into the kitchen. In their roundness,

he sees his mother's breasts. In their smoothness,
he finds the consoling touch of her hands.
Mother, mother, he cries, and flings himself
on the tomatoes. Forget about the knife, the fork,
the pinch of salt. Try to imagine the filial
starvation, think of his ravenous kisses.

These are the first days of fall. The wind
at evening smells of roads still to be traveled,
while the sound of leaves blowing across the lawns
is like an unsettled feeling in the blood,
the desire to get in a car and just keep driving.
A man and a dog descend their front steps.
The dog says, Let's go downtown and get crazy drunk.
Let's tip over all the trash cans we can find.
This is how dogs deal with the prospect of change.
But in his sense of the season, the man is struck
by the oppressiveness of his past, how his memories
which were shifting and fluid have grown more solid
until it seems he can see remembered faces
caught up among the dark places in the trees.
The dog says, Let's pick up some girls and just
rip off their clothes. Let's dig holes everywhere.
Above his house, the man notices wisps of cloud
crossing the face of the moon. Like in a movie,
he says to himself, a movie about a person
leaving on a journey. He looks down the street
to the hills outside of town and finds the cut
where the road heads north. He thinks of driving
on that road and the dusty smell of the car
heater, which hasn't been used since last winter.
The dog says, Let's go down to the diner and sniff
people's legs. Let's stuff ourselves on burgers.
In the man's mind, the road is empty and dark.
Pine trees press down to the edge of the shoulder,
where the eyes of animals, fixed in his headlights,
shine like small cautions against the night.
Sometimes a passing truck makes his whole car shake.
The dog says, Let's go to sleep. Let's lie down
by the fire and put our tails over our noses.
But the man wants to drive all night, crossing

one state line after another, and never stop
until the sun creeps into his rearview mirror.
Then he'll pull over and rest awhile before
starting again, and at dusk he'll crest a hill
and there, filling a valley, will be the lights
of a city entirely new to him.
But the dog says, Let's just go back inside.
Let's not do anything tonight. So they
walk back up the sidewalk to the front steps.
How is it possible to want so many things
and still want nothing. The man wants to sleep
and wants to hit his head again and again
against a wall. Why is it all so difficult?
But the dog says, Let's go make a sandwich.
Let's make the tallest sandwich anyone's ever seen.
And that's what they do and that's where the man's
wife finds him, staring into the refrigerator
as if into the place where the answers are kept—
the ones telling why you get up in the morning
and how it is possible to sleep at night,
answers to what comes next and how to like it.

MARSYAS, MIDAS AND THE BARBER

The duel between Marsyas and Apollo was one of those
historical things—flute versus strings, peasants
versus roving noblemen. Marsyas had found the pipes
near a stream and since they almost seemed to play
themselves he gave himself up to the pleasure. Then,
when he saw he had talent, he thought, Why not
be tops? He was a domesticated satyr with ambitions,
a little fellow who wanted to be a big fellow,
whose one admirer in high places was King Midas,
who liked his low jokes and easy way with women.
Nobody had looked at him until he found the flute,
he was too fat, too lazy. Even with the flute they only
paid attention when he played, so he played all the time,
until Apollo appeared and said, You must think you're
pretty hot. Even then Marsyas couldn't stay shut up,
mostly because the peasants kept bobbing their heads,
begging him to show this big fellow just what a hot
ticket he really was, and even Midas nodded
encouragingly and backed the local boy over the star.
But it should be noted that the contest that followed
had nothing to do with music. It was all about
brainpower, and there Apollo beat him flat. Whatever
made Marsyas think he could sing and play the pipes
at the same time? Could he sing with his nose, blow
with his ears? And so he lost both the contest
and his skin, which Apollo ripped from his body
like a sock from a foot. Then it was Midas's turn
to bear the brunt of divine attention with the god
standing above him asking unpleasant questions.
Did Midas really think Marsyas the better musician?
Shuffling his feet, scratching his chin, Midas
had never been known for the wisdom of his decisions—
just look at his trouble with food turning to gold.
But, yes, despite threats and dire consequences

he would stand up for Marsyas; the flute had defeated
the lyre. But Apollo had no use for Midas's loyalty
and so the mortal's insolence was ironically punished.
You think you've got good ears, buster? Try hearing
with these. How dreadful to find his once normal ears
had been turned into a pair of floppy ones covered
with silky brown fur. Tugging at one as it dangled
near the level of his chin, Midas probably caught
a glimpse of his future—bleak for himself, funny
for everyone else. Was it worth it? Did he recant?
If given a second chance, would he shout, Marsyas,
what a bum, no tact, no talent and no technique!
But lucky for us history gives no second chances
or consider the bravery that might go unrepeated—
Horatio dodging the bridge, Crockett missing the Alamo.
The necessity is to act from your essential nature,
and Midas, though foolish, was loyal. Even Marsyas,
a near nobody, was fated to be true to his instrument.
And Midas's barber—you see how these stories descend
to their lowest denominators—even the barber,
who had been warned to keep his mouth shut or else,
was at a loss to obey, being naturally talkative.
How could he be expected to keep such a secret?
So he spoke it to a hole in the ground and soon
all the grass was saying, King Midas has asses' ears.
At the very moment of his execution, did the barber
still think he'd ever had the ability to keep silent?
And Midas, now that the entire country knew about
his unfortunate deformity, could he stand up
and tell the world that Marsyas was a no-talent bum?
And Marsyas, as he wandered through the woods
wondering why he had so few friends, when he saw
the flute and picked it up, if somebody smart
had rushed up to tell him the nature of his future,

would he have dropped the flute and turned aside?
He was a little artist who wanted to be a big artist.
Had he been able to see his skin nailed to a tree
would he have denied the dancers, the cheering crowds
in favor of a long life and anonymity forever?

Waking, I look at you sleeping beside me.
It is early and the baby in her crib
has begun her conversation with the gods
that direct her, cooing and making small hoots.
Watching you, I see how your face bears the signs
of our time together—for each objective
description, there is the romantic; for each
scientific fact, there's the subjective truth—
this line was caused by days at a microscope,
this from when you thought I no longer loved you.
Last night a friend called to say that he intends
to move out; so simple, he and his wife splitting
like a cell into two separate creatures.
What would happen if we divided ourselves?
As two colors blend on a white pad, so we
have become a third color; or better,
as a wire bites into the tree it surrounds,
so we have grown together. Can you believe
how frightening I find this, to know I have
no life except with you? It's almost enough
to make me destroy it just to protest it.
Always we seemed perched on the brink of chaos.
But today there's just sunlight and the baby's
chatter, her wonder at the way light dances
on the wall. How lucky to be ignorant,
to greet joy without a trace of suspicion,
to take that first step without worrying what
comes trailing after, as night trails after day,
or winter summer, or confusion where all
seemed clear and each moment was its own reward.

My daughter baby Clio lies on her back
on the sheepskin rug, jerking her arms and feet
like a turtle stuck upside down in the dirt
struggling to get up. But here there is no threat,
I tell myself. The room is benign and I
act for the best. She is just contentedly
wriggling. It is nothing like a turtle flipped
over while two or three crows sidle closer,
eager to pluck her soft parts. The room is safe
and I direct my life to keep it like that.
How much is this a fiction I believe in?
We are forced to live in a place without walls
and I build her shelter with bits of paper.
The ever-attentive beaks surround us. These
birds are her future—face of a teacher, face
of a thief, one with the face of her father.

THE GENERAL AND THE TANGO SINGER

Some people put their trust in art, others
believe in murder. Each can be in error.
Take the example of the general and the tango
singer who go to a restaurant for dinner.
They are both big men and they are starving,
so they order a five-course meal beginning
with clams casino. Then they settle down to discuss
the nature of beauty. For the tango singer,
beauty means submission to the rule of objects.
For the general, it means force—the beauty
of a mailed fist. Suddenly the owner
bursts through the door shouting, Fire, Fire!
The stockroom is in flames. He must get help.
Look no farther, says the general, I can put
the fire out. And if he can't, says the tango
singer, then I can—bring us the turtle soup.
The two friends eat the soup and talk about truth.
For the general, truth is the ability
to whip your ideas forward to victory.
For the singer, it means knowing when to give in.
The owner appears again; the whole back
of the restaurant is burning. Forget it,
says the tango singer, we'll fix it in a minute—
bring us the salmon soufflé. And more wine,
says the general, we need more wine. They eat
and drink and talk about art. For the singer,
art consists of synthesis and compromise.
For the general, it's a total assault
on the senses—something like a punch in the nose.
The owner again comes running. He is crying.
The fire has reached the kitchen. There'll be
no more food tonight. With the air of men
for whom duty is a harsh mistress, the general
and tango singer prepare to put out the blaze.

Such a nuisance, says the general. Such a bore,
says the tango singer. The fire appears at the door.
Talk about starving, roars the fire, I am really
ravenous. The general tells everyone
to stand back. Then he takes out his pistol
and shoots six bullets into the flames.
Yum, yum, says the fire, I adore hot lead.
Now it's my turn, says the tango singer.
He begins to sing one of his very own songs—
When my baby ran off with Big Leo,
I cut off her feet and threw them in the trash.
The music splashes over the fire, which
gobbles up each note before sweeping forward
through the restaurant, devouring tables,
chairs, the white tablecloths, devouring
even the plates. Everyone rushes out
to the street. The restaurant is destroyed.
You said you could save it, cries the owner.
The general and tango singer shrug their shoulders.
That was not a real fire, they say, a real
fire would have begged for mercy. We cannot
be held responsible for frauds. The general
and the tango singer stroll off down the street.
Did you see how it hesitated when I shot it?
Did you see how it paused when I sang?
Both are very pleased. They talk about the confused
state of the world. When will it ever get better?
These problems won't be solved in our lifetime,
says the general, yet how fortunate for those future
generations to have their road made clear. Yes,
says the tango singer, that lucky time will come
like a gentle caress. I beg to differ, says
the general, it will come like a bust in the jaw.
Behind them the fire listens to their talk

as it picks over the restaurant as if over
a plate of bones. It knows how the future will come,
no one knows better. And if its mouth were not
too full to speak, it would gladly tell. How sweet
will be that future time when night will burn
as bright as day, when each cold corner receives
the precious gift of warmth and even the smallest
fire toddles off to dreamland on a full stomach.

Because the moon burns a bright orange,
because their memories beat them like flails,
because even in death it is possible
to take only so much, because the night
watchman has slipped out for a drink,
the dead decide to have a party. Helter-skelter,
they hurry to the center of the graveyard,
clasp hands and attack the possibility
of pleasure. How brave to play the clarinet
when your fingers fall off. How persevering to dance
when your feet keep fleeing into the tall grass.
How courageous to sing when your tongue flops down
on the stage and you must stop to stick it back.
And what does she sing, this chanteuse of the night,
Melancholy Baby? I Got Plenty of Nothing?

Where we have come from we'll soon forget.
Where we are going is the dust at our feet.
Where we are now is the best we can expect.

Slim pickings, says a crow to his buddy.
Just wait 'til the world flips over, says the other,
then we'll eat until our stomachs burst.
In a nearby bar the night watchman says, They can't
keep me down, I'm going places, I got plans.
The bartender yawns and glances from the window.
Some great bird is flapping across the face of the moon.
He thinks, Whatever happened to Jenny Whatshername?
Car crash, cancer, killer in the night? He remembers
once watching her pee in the woods, how she just
squatted down and pulled up her pink dress.
For fifteen cents she let him see her crack.
So white it looked, the wound that would never heal;
then how pink when she had delicately

spread it apart with two fingers. Excitedly,
he galloped through the woods waving a stick,
hitting trees, clumps of earth; seek marauders,
Indians, pirates to kill just to protect her.

SPIRITUAL CHICKENS

A man eats a chicken every day for lunch,
and each day the ghost of another chicken
joins the crowd in the dining room. If he could
only see them! Hundreds and hundreds of spiritual
chickens, sitting on chairs, tables, covering
the floor, jammed shoulder to shoulder. At last
there is no more space and one of the chickens
is popped back across the spiritual plain to the earthly.
The man is in the process of picking his teeth.
Suddenly there's a chicken at the end of the table,
strutting back and forth, not looking at the man
but knowing he is there, as is the way with chickens.
The man makes a grab for the chicken but his hand
passes right through her. He tries to hit the chicken
with a chair and the chair passes through her.
He calls in his wife but she can see nothing.
This is his own private chicken, even if he
fails to recognize her. How is he to know
this is a chicken he ate seven years ago
on a hot and steamy Wednesday in July,
with a little tarragon, a little sour cream?
The man grows afraid. He runs out of his house
flapping his arms and making peculiar hops
until the authorities take him away for a cure.
Faced with the choice between something odd
in the world or something broken in his head,
he opts for the broken head. Certainly,
this is safer than putting his opinions
in jeopardy. Much better to think he had
imagined it, that he had made it happen.
Meanwhile, the chicken struts back and forth
at the end of the table. Here she was, jammed in
with the ghosts of six thousand dead hens, when
suddenly she has the whole place to herself.

Even the nervous man has disappeared. If she
had a brain, she would think she had caused it.
She would grow vain, egotistical, she would
look for someone to fight, but being a chicken
she can just enjoy it and make little squawks,
silent to all except the man who ate her,
who is far off banging his head against a wall
like someone trying to repair a leaky vessel,
making certain that nothing unpleasant gets in
or nothing of value falls out. How happy
he would have been to be born a chicken,
to be of good use to his fellow creatures
and rich in companionship after death.
As it is he is constantly being squeezed
between the world and his idea of the world.
Better to have a broken head—why surrender
his corner on truth?—better just to go crazy.

Here comes the woman who wears the plastic prick
hooked to a string around her waist, the man who
puts girls' panties like a beanie on his head,
the chicken molester, the lady who likes Great Danes,
the boy who likes sheep, the old fellow who likes
to watch turkeys dance on the top of a hot stove,
the bicycle-seat sniffer, grasshopper muncher,
the bubbles-in-the-bath biter—they all meet
each night at midnight and, oh lord, they bowl.
From twelve to six they take it out on the pins
as they discuss their foibles with their friends.
I'm trying to cut down, says the woman who nibbles
the tails of mice. I've thrown away my Zippo, says
the man who sticks matches between people's toes.
There is nothing that can't become a pleasure
if one lets it, and so they bowl. They think
of that oddly handsome German shepherd face
and they bowl. Their hands quiver at the thought
of jamming their fingers in a car door
and they bowl. These are the heroes, these
grocers and teachers and postmen and plumbers.
They bring snapshots of themselves and Scotch tape,
then fix their photos to the pins and they bowl.
They focus on their faces at the end of the alley
and they bowl. They see the hunger in their eyes,
the twist of anticipation in their lips, and oh
they bowl—bowl to remember, bowl to forget,
as the pins with their own bruised faces explode
from midnight to six. While in those explosions
of wood, in which each pin describes an exact arc,
they feast on those moments when the world seems to stop
and everything conspires to push some fleeting
beauty—ripening peach or blossoming rose—
to the queer brink of perfection, where it flames,
flickers, fades, and is never perfect again.

WHITE PIG

A family decides to have a party.
It is a graduation or birthday.
The father buys a little white pig,
just enough for his wife and six kids
with something left over for someone special.
The father has no idea how to kill a pig
but he meets a man in a bar who says,
Don't worry, I have killed hundreds of pigs.
He is a young man with a big smile.
On the day of the party, the young man arrives
early in the morning. I have no knife,
he says. And he takes the bread knife
and begins sharpening it on a stone.
He sharpens the knife and drinks brandy.
The white pig trots through the house.
The children have tied a blue ribbon
around her neck and the baby's blue bonnet
on her head. The pig thinks she is very cute.
She lets the children feed her cookies and
ride on her back. The man with the smile keeps
sharpening and drinking, sharpening and drinking.
The morning is getting late. Why don't you
do something? says the father. The pig pokes
her head around the door, then scampers away.
The young man drinks more brandy. It is nearly noon.
Why don't you kill the pig? says the father.
He wants to get it over with. The young man
looks sullenly at the floor, looks sullenly
at the father and his neat little house.
He gets to his feet and sways back and forth.
You're drunk, says the father. The young man
raises the knife. Not too drunk to kill a pig,
he shouts. He stumbles out of the kitchen.
Where's that bitch of a pig? he shouts.
The pig is upstairs with the children.

I'm ready, says the young man, now I'm
really ready. He rushes up the stairs
and into the room where the pig is playing.
You whore! he shouts. He dives at the pig
and stabs her in the leg. The pig squeals.
Outside, shouts the father, you have to kill her
outside! The pig is terrified and rushes
around the room squealing and bleeding on the rug.
The blue bonnet slips down over one eye.
You slut! shouts the young man. He leaps
at the pig and stabs her in the shoulder.
The children are screaming. The parents are shouting.
The young man chases the pig through the whole house.
You whore, you slut, you little Jew of a pig!
Outside, outside! shouts the father. He knows
the rules, knows how a pig should be killed.
For the pig, it's a nightmare. The blue bonnet
has slipped down over both eyes and she can
hardly see. She squeals over and over. There is
no sound in the world like that one.
At last the young man traps the pig
in the laundry room. He leaps on her.
You black bitch of a pig! he shouts. He stabs
the pig over and over. The children
stand in the doorway crying. The father
is crying. His wife hides in the bedroom.
What a great party this has turned out to be.
Finally the pig is dead. The young man
holds her up by the hind legs. Again he is
smiling. This is one dead pig! he shouts.
He has probably stabbed her over two hundred times.
The pig looks like a piece of Swiss cheese.
The young man carries the pig to the kitchen
and begins to butcher her, then he helps

to cook the pig. All afternoon the house
is full of wonderful smells. The children
hide in their bedrooms. The mother and father
scrub and scrub to clean up the blood. At last
the pig is ready to be eaten. It is a party,
maybe a graduation or birthday.
The children refuse to come downstairs.
The mother and father don't feel hungry.
The young man sits at the table by himself.
He is served by a neighborhood girl hired
to wash the dishes. He eats and eats. Tasty,
he says, there's nothing so tasty as young pig.
He drinks wine and laughs. He stuffs himself
on the sweet flesh of the little white pig.
Late at night he is still eating. The children
are in bed, the parents are in bed. The father
lies on his back and listens to the young man singing—
hunting songs, marching songs, songs of journeys
through dark places, songs of conquest and revenge.

The lives of Greeks in the old days were deep,
mysterious, and often lead to questions like,
Just what was wrong with Ariadne anyway, that's
what I'd like to know? She would have done
anything for that rascally Theseus, and what
did he do but sneak out in the night and row
back to his ship with black sails. Let's get
the heck out of here, he muttered to his crew,
and they leaned on their oars as he went whack-
whack on the whacking block—a human metronome
of adventure and ill fortune. She was King Minos's
daughter and had helped Theseus kill the king's
pet monster, her half-brother, so possibly
he didn't like feeling beholden—people might
think he wasn't tough. But certainly he'd spent
his life knocking chips off shoulders and flattening
any fellow reckless enough to step across a line
drawn in the dust. If you wanted a punch thrown,
Theseus was just the cowboy to throw it. I'm only
happy when hitting and scratching, he'd told Ariadne
that first night. So he'd been the logical choice
to sail down from Athens to Crete to stop this
nonsense of a tribute of virgins for some
monster to eat. Those Cretans called it eating but
Theseus thought himself no fool and liked a virgin
as well as the next man. Not that he could have got
into the labyrinth without Ariadne's help, or out
either for that matter. As for the Minotaur, lounging
on his couch, nibbling grapes and sipping wine while
a troop of ex-virgins fluttered to his beck and call,
Theseus must have scared the horns right off him,
slamming back the door and standing there in his lion-
skin suit and waving that ugly club. The poor beast
might have had a stroke had there been time before

Theseus pummeled him into the earth. Then, with
Ariadne's help, Theseus escaped, and soon after he
ditched her on an island and sailed off in his ship
with black sails, which returns us to the question:
Just what was wrong with Ariadne anyway?
But nobody like Theseus likes a smart girl, always
telling him to dress warmly and eat plenty of fiber.
She was one of those people who are never in doubt.
Had he sharpened his sword, tied his sandals?
Without her, of course, he would have never escaped
the labyrinth. Why hadn't he thought of that trick
with the ball of yarn? But as he looked down
at her sleeping form, this woman who was already
carrying his child, maybe he thought of their
future together, how she would correctly foretell
the mystery or banality behind each locked door.
So probably he shook his head and said, Give me
a dumb girl any day, and crept back to his ship
and sailed away. Of course Ariadne was revenged.
She would have told him to change the sails,
to take down the black ones, put up the white.
She would have reminded him that his father,
the king of Athens, was waiting on a high cliff
scanning the Aegean for Theseus's returning ship,
white for victory, black for defeat. She would
have said how his father would see the black sails,
how the grief for the supposed death of his one son
would destroy him. But Theseus and his men had
brought out the wine and were cruising a calm sea
in a small boat filled to the brim with ex-virgins.
Who could have blamed him? Until he heard the distant
scream and his head shot up to see the black sails
and he knew. The girls disappeared, the ship grew
quiet except for the lap-lap of the water. Staring

toward the spot where his father had tumbled
headfirst into the Aegean, Theseus understood
he would always be a stupid man with a thick stick,
scratching his forehead long after the big event.
But think, does he change his mind, turn back
the ship, hunt up Ariadne and beg her pardon?
Far better to be stupid by himself than smart
because she'd been tugging on his arm; better
to live in the eternal present with a boatload
of ex-virgins than in that dark land of consequences
promised by Ariadne, better to live like any one of us,
thinking to outwit the darkness, but knowing
it will catch us, that we will be surprised like
the Minotaur on his couch when the door slams back
and the hired gun of our personal destruction bursts
upon us, upsetting the good times and scaring the girls.
Better to be ignorant, to go into the future as into
a long tunnel, without ball of yarn or clear direction,
to tiptoe forward like any fool or saint or hero,
jumpy, full of second thoughts, and bravely unprepared.

for Stratis Haviaras

WHITE THIGHS

White thighs like slices of white cake—
three pre-teenage girls on a subway
talking excitedly about what they will
see and do and buy downtown, while near them
a man stares, then pulls back to look
at the slash and jab of the graffiti.
He sees himself as trying to balance
on the peak of a steep metal roof
but once again he turns to watch
the girls in their grown-up dresses,
their eye shadow and painted mouths. How
white the skin must be on the insides
of their thighs. He can almost taste
their heat and he imagines his teeth
pressed to the humid flesh until once more
he jerks back his head like yanking
a dog on a leash, until he sees his face
in the glass, gray and middle-aged. The night,
he thinks, the night—meaning not simply
nighttime but those hours before dawn
when he feels his hunger as if it were
a great hulking creature in the hallway
outside his door, some beast of darkness.
And again he feels his head beginning
to twist on its hateful stalk. White thighs—
to trip or slip on that steep metal roof:
his final capitulation to the dark.

These are days of sickness and forgetting.
A man stands in line at a whorehouse.
Tonight there is something special.
The other girls paint their nipples black
and spit on the men waiting in line.
The man keeps moving forward. He reaches
a room where a woman is lying on her back.
What is so special about this?
A telescope is tucked up between
her legs, tucked right up inside her.
One by one the men go to her,
kneel down between her fat white thighs.
At last it's the man's turn.
Kneeling down on a blue rug,
he leans forward between the whore's legs.
He puts his eye to the telescope.
Shortly, he sees himself as he was
years before, sees himself as a small child.
His parents are giving him a bath.
They are talking and laughing. They lift him
from the tub, dry him with warm towels.
His father carries him to the bedroom.
He snuggles down between cool white sheets.
Someone slaps him on the back. Come on,
you son of a pig, your time's up. The whore
snaps her fingers at the next in line.
The man goes downstairs to the street.
It has begun to rain, great black drops
that smash and break on the pavement.
The man has a hundred friends he could visit
but to each one he says no.

THE NIHILIST

He was depressed so he made something.
He created light but it made nothing better.
It burned his face; it hurt his eyes.
So he made water to soothe and refresh him
and the light flickered on miles of blue water
but it wasn't enough. I'm tired, he said,
I need a place to sit. So he made earth.
The light is too bright, he said, I need shade.
So he made trees. I need something beautiful,
he said. So he made the moon and stars, and saw
how they glittered and filled the night sky,
but they made nothing better. I'm bored, he said,
I need toys. So he made birds and every kind
of creeping thing. I need servants, he said,
creatures to do as I tell them. So he made
men and women and watched them scurry across
the earth eager to please him and do his bidding.
But their desires bored him, they filled him
with exhaustion. I'll make them move faster,
he said. So he gave them discontent and hunger.
Then he set Death as his captain over them
and watched them march around on the earth
until he wanted to laugh and slap his knee
but it wasn't enough, the vacancy stayed within him.
He looked at what he had made—the light and water,
the little human creatures. What a mess it was,
what a complication of celestial doodling.
And to the eager, those with the biggest appetite,
he said, You can keep it, you can do with it
what you will. Then he lifted himself up to the stars,
those baubles of light, and gently he set his face
among them so it shone forth with its teeth
and dark eyes, its vast brow of discontent.
Then he began to scrape and rub at it

so that his greatest creation would be his own
obliteration, and his face blinked out like a dying spark,
leaving the human creatures running back and forth,
craning their necks and calling out the many names
they had given him, although he still hung there
had anyone the ability to see him. That's his face,
that vacancy between the stars, that dark place
filling the sky as water fills a cup, or a room
without people, no tables or chairs or pictures
on the walls. This is an empty room, you say.
Wrong, wrong again. Listen carefully, hear the laughter.

Betting on how many leaves cover a birch,
then counting them. Betting how many Buicks
drive past the graveyard in a single week,
then doing the sums. Betting how many crows fly
north-south as opposed to east-west in a single month,
then adding them up. Such are the memories of the dead.
Holidays, with their burden of memories,
are even worse. Christmas, Easter, George
Washington's birthday, even Halloween
is a time for weeping and the gnashing
of those few remaining teeth. One Thanksgiving
a turkey fell from the back of a speeding truck,
staggered into the graveyard and collapsed.
The dead stood round and watched. When the turkey
revived, it had eyes only for the maggots which
the dead wear as a socialite wears her jewels.
For a turkey, maggots mean feasting and pleasure, which
is the difference between a living and dead
Thanksgiving. In life, a dozen friends surround
one dead bird. In death, one living turkey attempts
to round up a dozen dead . . . Were they friends?
No, in death there are only acquaintances.

Luckily, a young man was hurrying by and he
saw the turkey, grabbed it and wrung its neck.
How simple are these problems for the living.
He was on his way to his parents' for dinner.
They were poor. It was the old story. No
turkey for them, maybe hamburger or chicken.
Now all was changed. He would toss the turkey
down on the table and his father would grin,
in that way he used to, and reach out and very
lightly he would tap his son's jaw with his fist.
As the son hurried toward this certain pleasure,

he thought of how his father used to carry him
up to bed, the rough feel of his father's bristles
against his cheek and the smell of hair oil
and sweat. How long ago that seemed. What train
was carrying him such a distance from that time,
and what dark fields would be his destination?

What is the division between good intention
and best behavior? Or rather, let's say it's
a fence, a ditch, some sort of barrier, since
many times we stand on one side looking over
at the creature we should be but aren't. And this,
it seems, is where we are often most human,
lost in the country between Want To and Can't.

A man is hitchhiking. The devil picks him up.
Where to? says the devil, who is in disguise
and looks like an old lady in a blue straw hat
who just happens to be driving a Ferrari.
My father is sick, I must see him, says
the man, who's never been in a Ferrari before.
This one is red and very fast. The world
flies by. Apparently by accident, they zoom past
the father's house. The man doesn't speak.
After a few more blocks, the devil makes
a U-turn and drives him back. That was
a real treat, says the man. Inside, he finds
that two weeks have gone by. His father
is dead and buried. Everyone is disappointed.
Even the police have been out looking. What
can I say, says the man, I guess I let you down.
The phone rings. It's his wife, who tells him,
Come home right away. The man hitchhikes home.
The devil picks him up in his bright red Ferrari.
By now the man is suspicious but as they
whiz by his house he doesn't make a peep.
He leans back and feels the sun on his brow.
When the devil gets him home, two more weeks
have disappeared. His wife has moved out lock,
stock and barrel; the house is empty except
for the telephone, which begins to ring. Now

it's his mother who is sick. I'll be right over,
says the man. The Ferrari is waiting at the curb.
The man doesn't hesitate. He leaps inside.
He leans back. Once more the wind is in his hair.
He wallows in soft leather as in a warm bath.
But this time he knows the score, knows the driver
isn't a little old lady, knows they will zoom
past his mother's house, that he won't protest.
He knows his mother will die, that he'll miss
the funeral. He searches his soul for just
a whisper of guilt, but if it's there, it's been
drowned out by the purr of the big motor.
Am I really so weak? the man asks himself.
And he peers across that metaphorical ditch
to the sort of person he would like to be,
but he can't make the jump, bridge the gap.
Why can't I fight off temptation? he asks.
He sees his future as clear as a map
with all the bad times circled in red.
He knows that as crisis is piled on crisis
he will find the Ferrari waiting at the curb,
and that no matter how hard he tries to resist
he will succumb at last to the wish to feel
the wind riffle his hair, the touch of leather,
to be lulled by the gentle vibration of the motor
as life slips by in a succession of short rides.

When are we satisfied or get what we want,
when do we speak the truth of our feelings?
A man has been rude to the rich and powerful.
Magicians are called in. After much talk,
they decide to put him inside a tree. The man
wakes up. It's dark. He discovers he's trapped
inside a black walnut but it takes many years
to understand this. He becomes accustomed
to the touch of birds' feet, the touch of wind
and change of seasons, but to his suffering
and sense of loss he becomes accustomed
never. Oh, how he misses his loved ones.
Then, by good fortune, a local sculptor cuts
down the black walnut to make a figurehead
for a nearby tavern. The man trapped inside
believes that in this new shape he might
at last be able to express his pain and
frustrated longing. Stoically, he endures
the tap of the hammer, bite of the chisel.
Although the sculptor is one of the world's
ten million bad artists, he successfully
turns the tree into a mermaid with golden
hair, pendulous breasts and scarlet nipples.
The man inside looks out through the mermaid's
bright blue eyes and in a mirror he sees how
his suffering has been transformed into
the alluring invitation of the mermaid's curves.
The sculptor has taken the man's desire
for his wife and changed it into a twinkle
in the mermaid's eye. He has taken the man's
pride and turned it into the mermaid's grin.
He has taken his rebellion and reshaped it
into the upward thrust of the mermaid's breasts.
How easily does artifice transform true feeling.

Yet how strongly does feeling continue to struggle.
Months pass, years go by. On windy nights,
the mermaid swings from her double chain
so the links chafe and rub, making a sound
like a creaking door, and in that noise the man
trapped in the wood puts all his unhappiness.
What a gloomy sound, say the men returning from work,
mechanics and carpenters, the men from the mines,
and they hurry into the tavern and order their beer,
and there among the smoke and laughter, one lifts
his glass and drinks to the future. But as he speaks
the word, he hears the creaking of the chain
and briefly he sees himself feeling his way
down a tunnel deep in the mountain, lost with
no light and no friends and no sense of an end
to his own unique but not uncommon story.

How difficult to be an angel.
In order to forgive, they have no memory.
In order to be good, they are always forgetting.
How else could heaven be run? Still,
it needs to be full of teachers and textbooks
imported from God's own basement, since only
in hell is memory exact. In one classroom,
a dozen angels scratch their heads as their teacher
displays the cross-section of a human skull,
saying, Here is sadness, here
the anger, here's where laughter is kept.
And the angels think, How strange, and take notes
and would temper their forgiveness if it weren't
all forgotten by the afternoon. Sometimes
a group flies down to earth with their teacher,
who wants them to study a living example, and
this evening they find a man lying in a doorway
in an alley in Detroit. They stand around
chewing their pencils as their teacher says,
This is the bottle he drinks from when he
wants to forget, this is the Detroit Tigers
T-shirt he wears whenever he's sad, this is
the electric kazoo he plays in order to weep.
And the angels think, How peculiar, and wonder
whether to temper their forgiveness or just
let it ride, which really doesn't matter since
they forget the question as soon as it's asked.
But their muttering wakes the man in the doorway,
who looks to see a flock of doves departing
over the trash cans. And because he dreamt
of betrayal and pursuit, of defeat in battle,
the death of friends, he heaves a bottle at them
and it breaks under a streetlight so the light
reflects on its hundred broken pieces with such

a multicolored twinkling that the man laughs.
From their place on a brick wall, the angels
watch and one asks, What good are they? Then
others take up the cry, What good are they,
what good are they? But as fast as they articulate
the question it's forgotten and their teacher,
a minor demon, returns with them to heaven.
But the man, still chuckling, sits in his doorway,
and the rats in their dumpsters hear this sound
like stones rattling or metal banging together,
and they see how the man is by himself without
food or companions, without work or family
or a real bed for his body. They creep back
to their holes and practice little laughs
that sound like coughing or a dog throwing up
as once more they uselessly try to imitate
the noise the hairless make when defeated.

Immediately on emerging from the dark tunnel
to hell, Orpheus began to kick at the earth
and curse Eurydice for her betrayal. She knew
he was weak. She knew he could refuse her nothing.
Why had she begged to see his face? Squatting down,
he pressed his mouth to the mouth of the hole.
Why have I let you break my heart? he shouted.
He thought of her smug, self-satisfied smile
when he had turned and taken his last look at her,
knowing they were lost, that their story was over.
Still, for weeks he lingered around that hole
in the earth with its smell of decay and the vast
murmur of the dead like the murmur of the sea,
unable to eat, unable to play the lyre.
Other women came, but he ignored them.
They offered themselves, but he refused them.
See us as Eurydice, they asked. Impossible,
he said, you are too different. Show us, they said.
He described how her hair fell over one shoulder.
Like that, he said, but yours is the wrong color.
Show us, they answered. So they changed the color
of their hair. Then he taught them how to dress,
how to walk, how to make up their faces until
once more she stood before him and his grief
overswept his heart. Come with us, they said.
But Orpheus still wasn't ready. Walk after me,
he told them, beg me to look at your faces.
So they began their journey across the country—
Orpheus first, then the dozen Thracian women.
Orpheus, they cried, look at us, look at our faces.
But Orpheus felt no temptation to turn.
He raised his lyre and began to play.
He strode along and the women hurried to catch up,
stumbling and hurting themselves on the stones.
Orpheus, they cried, turn and look at us.

We are Eurydice. Louder, he said, cry louder.
The women raised their voices and he pretended
not to hear them. He was filled with confidence.
I'll go back, he thought, I'll return to hell.

What else could the women do but destroy him?
They were sick to death of his endless strumming.
They grew berserk and before he could say Stop
or There has been a mistake, they tore him apart
and threw the pieces into the River Hebrus. How
soothing the silence felt. How wonderful to view
the horizon without the insult of his indifferent back.
They returned to their lives, got married, grew fat.
They forgot about Orpheus and the indiscretions
of their youth, or perhaps they remembered a time
when there had been a light or maybe a noise
and it had grown too loud or maybe too bright.
Whatever the case, they had brushed it aside.
Orpheus's lyre washed up on the shores of Lesbos,
where it was put in a temple for safekeeping.
One night, years later, a wealthy young man
crept into the temple meaning to play a few songs.
He had a girlfriend he wanted to impress.
He had no sense of the danger, no sense
of the power of the instrument. He touched
the strings. Eurydice, they cried, Eurydice!
The sound was like a wind that flattens wheat.
It swept through the city, driving animals crazy.
From every street, dogs raced toward the temple,
snarling and biting themselves in frenzy,
scrambling over each other's backs through the doorway.
As the Thracian women had killed Orpheus,
so the dogs devoured the foolish young man.
What else could they have done, being earthborn,
but slaughter what had pricked their creature hearts?

THE PARTY

You enter a room—Indians, Iraqis,
Indonesians, and at the kitchen table
a woman in a white blouse. You talk to her.
The host is a poet from Peru. His guests
are writers except for this woman, who studies
biology. For some reason you never
remember, you talk to her about reality
and imagination in the poetry
of Wallace Stevens. At one point you feel like
reaching out, touching your fingers to her cheek,
and this surprises you so much that you pull back.
This is your wife, the woman you finally marry.
One night years later you stare at the long cut
in her belly, out of which your only child
was brought into this world. You two, man and wife,
have had much trouble—a life like sandpaper
against the skin—and the cut in her belly
is like a symbol of all that has happened,
as if your heart or hers were torn from that spot.
Yet often, seeing her, you still desire
to reach out, lay your fingers against her cheek.
You remember in Stevens the words "Let be
be finale of seem." You told her this meant
that what exists is more important than what
seems to exist. The scar on your wife's belly
resembles six inches of comic strip lightning,
sometimes it strikes one way, sometimes another.
Always it is such a confusion, trying
to know what is real and what imagined.
The party was shortly after Thanksgiving.
The year had begun badly, then got better,
to become a time when life seemed easy.
Even the weather stayed mild, with marigolds
outside the door until into December.
Then the whole mess began to tilt. Light to dark,

you feel pushed from light to dark. Often it seems
the wish to touch her cheek is the one reason
you stay together, that stubborn desire
that gets left over when all the rest collapses.

STREETLIGHT

The streetlight from my parents' bed at night split
so perfectly into four branches of light
that at five I knew one could surely be climbed.
Lying in their bed, I pictured myself perched
on that crossbar of radiance, ready to
shinny up its cold flame to discover what?
That was the question, what happened at the top?
Again it seemed I had found another door
out of this world, another way to vanish.
But at five what was this need to disappear?—
as if I could creep under that bright curtain
of landscape to find out what the darkness was
or escape into a place from children's books,
a place important for being someplace else.
I think about that childhood self, so distant,
so foreign to any feeling that I have
it's as if he really broke free and might now
be wandering through some city, one of those kids
you pass on the street, who looks into your eyes
as if to say, I know you, I despise you,
you're nothing I desire—then looks away.

In the children's story of Ferdinand the Bull,
the bull gets off. He sits down, won't fight.
He manages to walk out of the ring without that
sharp poke of steel being shoved through
his back and deep into his heart. He returns
to the ranch and the sniffing of flowers.
But in real life, once the bull enters the ring,
then it's a certainty he will leave ignominiously,
dragged out by two mules while the attention of
the crowd rivets on the matador, who, if he's good,
holds up an ear, taken from the bull, and struts
around the ring, since it is his business to strut
as it is the bull's business to be dragged away.

.

It is the original eagerness of the bull which
takes one's breath. Suddenly he is there, hurtling
at the barrier, searching for something soft and
human to flick over his shoulder, trying to hook
his horn smack into the glittering belly
of the matador foolish enough to be there.
But there is a moment after the initial teasing
when the bull realizes that ridding the ring
of these butterfly creatures is not what
the afternoon is about. Sometimes it comes with
the first wrench of his back when the matador
turns him too quickly. Sometimes it comes
when the picador is driving his lance into
the bull's crest—the thick muscle between
the shoulder blades. Sometimes it comes when
the banderillos place their darts into that same
muscle and the bull shakes himself, trying to
free himself from that bright light in his brain.
Or it may come even later, when the matador

is trying to turn the bull again and again,
trying to wrench that same muscle which he uses
to hold up his head, to charge, to toss a horse.
It is the moment the bull stops and almost thinks,
when the eagerness disappears and the bull
realizes these butterflies can cause him pain,
when he turns to hunt out his querencia.

.

It sounds like care: querencia—and it means
affection or fondness, coming from *querer,*
to want or desire or love, but also to accept
a challenge as in a game, but also it means
a place chosen by a man or animal—querencia—
the place one cares most about, where one is
most secure, protected, where one feels safest.
In the ring, it may be a spot near the gate
or the place he was first hurt or where
the sand is wet or where there's a little blood,
his querencia, even though it looks like any
other part of the ring, except this is the spot
the bull picks as his home, the place he will
defend and keep returning to, the place where
he again decides to fight and lifts his head
despite the injured muscle, the place the matador
tries to keep him away from, where the bull
sensing defeat, is most dangerous and stubborn.

.

The passage through adulthood is the journey
through bravado, awareness and resignation
which the bull duplicates in his fifteen minutes
in the ring. As for the querencia, we all have
a place where we feel safest, even if it is only

the idea of a place, maybe an idea by itself,
the place that all our being radiates out from,
like an ideal of friendship or justice or perhaps
something simpler like the memory of a back porch
where we laughed a lot and how the setting sun
through the pine trees shone on the green chairs,
flickered off the ice cubes in our glasses.
We all have some spot in our mind which we
go back to from hospital bed, or fight with
husband or wife, or the wreckage of a life.
So the bull's decision is only the degree
to which he decides to fight, since the outcome
is already clear, since the mules are already
harnessed to drag his body across the sand.
Will he behave bravely and with dignity or
will he be fearful with his thick tongue lolling
from his mouth and the blood making his black
coat shiny and smooth? And the audience, no matter
how much it admires the matador, watches the bull
and tries to catch a glimpse of its own future.

.

At the end, each has a knowledge which is just
of inevitability, so the only true decision
is how to behave, like anyone supposedly—
the matador who tries to earn the admiration
of the crowd by displaying grace and bravery
in the face of peril, the bull who can't
be said to decide but who obeys his nature.
Probably, he has no real knowledge and,
like any of us, it's pain that teaches him
to be wary, so his only desire in defeat
is to return to that spot of sand, and even
when dying he will stagger toward his querencia

as if he might feel better there, could
recover there, take back his strength, win
the fight, stick that glittering creature to the wall,
while the matador tries to weaken that one muscle—
the animal all earnestness, the man all deceit—
until they come to that instant when the matador
decides the bull is ready and the bull appears
to submit by lowering his head, where the one
offers his neck and the other offers his belly,
and the matador's one hope is for a clean kill,
that the awful blade of the horn won't suddenly
rear up into the white softness of his groin.

One October in Barcelona I remember watching
a boy, an apprentice, lunge forward for the kill
and miss and miss again, how the bull would fling
the sword out of his back and across the ring,
and again stagger to his feet and shake himself,
and how the boy would try again and miss again,
until his assistant took a dagger and stabbed
repeatedly at the spinal cord as the bull tried
to drag himself forward to that place in the sand,
that querencia, as the crowd jeered and threw
their cushions and the matador stood back ashamed.
It was cold and the sun had gone down. The brightly
harnessed mules were already in the ring, and everyone
wanted to forget it and go home. How humiliating
it seemed and how hard the bull fought at the end
to drag himself to that one spot of safety, as if
that word could have any meaning in such a world.

Wheel of memory, wheel of forgetting, bitter
taste in the mouth—those who have been dead longest
group together in the center of the graveyard
facing inward. The sooner they become dust the better.
They pick at their flesh and watch it crumble,
they chip at their bones and watch them dissolve.
Do they have memories? Just shadows in the mind
like a hand passing between a candle and a wall.
Those who have been dead a lesser time stand
closer to the fence, but already they have started
turning away. Maybe they still have some sadness.
And what are their thoughts? Colors mostly,
sunset, sunrise, a burning house, someone waving
from the flames. Those who have recently died
line up against the fence facing outward,
watching the mailmen, deliverymen, the children
returning from school, listening to the church bells
dealing out the hours of the living day.
So arranged, the dead form a great spoked wheel—
such is the fiery wheel that rolls through heaven.

For the rats, nothing is more ridiculous
than the recently dead as they press against
the railing with their arms stuck between the bars.
Occasionally, one sees a friend, even a loved one.
Then what a shouting takes place as the dead
tries to catch the eye of the living. One actually
sees his wife waiting for a bus and he reaches out
so close that he nearly touches her yellow hair.
During life they were great lovers. Maybe
he should throw a finger at her, something
to attract her attention. Like a scarecrow
in a stiff wind, the dead husband waves his arms.
Is she aware of anything? Perhaps a slight breeze

on an otherwise still day, perhaps a smell of earth.
And what does she remember? Sometimes, when
she sits in his favorite chair or drinks a wine
that he liked, she will recall his face but
much faded, like a favorite dress washed too often.
And her husband, what does he think? As a piece
of crumpled paper burns within a fire,
so the thought of her burns within his brain.
And where is she going? These days she has taken
a new lover and she's going to his apartment. Even
as she waits, she sees herself sitting on his bed
as he unfastens the buttons of her blouse.
He will cup her breasts in his hands. A sudden
breeze will invade the room, making the dust
motes dance and sparkle as if each bright
spot were a single sharp-eyed intelligence,
as if the vast legion of the dead had come
with their unbearable jumble of envy and regret
to watch the man as he drops his head,
presses his mouth to the erect nipple.

FROM BODY TRAFFIC (1990)

THE BODY'S JOURNEY

Born, it's not good for much, a vehicle
stuck on its top, spinning its tires,
a pink VW Beetle or something resembling
a turtle. But it's cute so we keep it.

Soon it gets the hang of things and starts
to travel—first on its pudgy belly, then
on its beefy knees, until dangerously,
stubbornly, it wobbles along on two legs.

After that there's no holding it back—
think of the jazz it is able to dance
and the odd machinery it learns to drive:
unicycles, bathyspheres, spaceships,

as well as people. That really
is our main system of forward progression,
like a lemming or salmon—Toot, toot,
hey buddy, you're blocking the road!—

climbing over the bodies of all the folks
around us, until one can imagine a humongous
Himalaya of human flesh; and what a struggle
to this journey—a foot in this one's face,

one woman dragging herself up by the long
black tresses of another, an old man slamming
his cudgel against another old man's
bald spot, thousands scrambling to the top,

as millions of others sink within. And even
the losers, those near the bottom, keep
stamping on the rascals beneath them, just
to make sure they stay put. One wonders

at the fellow at the very bottom—saint or jerk,
cripple or coward—but perhaps there is no
absolute bottom, just as one can't imagine
an actual top, only fog at either end

with constant motion in between, everybody
frantic and all getting faster till one by one
they stumble from the crowd and each person's
private death greets him with a peck on the cheek.

But even then they keep traveling as death
climbs aboard each one, straddles each one
like a man paddling a canoe up a river and they
push off toward that place which nobody conquers.

Willows dabble their green hands in the water.
What memories alternate with what regrets,
what wistful hankerings, as the paddle repeats
its calming stroke and a loon warbles its cry?

THE BELLY

The belly puts on a bright red wig.
It puts on earmuffs and a pair of glasses.
It puts on a hat of crushed felt.
The belly thinks it's a brain.
It fits itself with a set of teeth.
I'm hungry, says the belly, I want more.
The belly decides to see the world.
It begins to travel. With its
perfect disguise it is invited everywhere.
The belly attends the meetings of bankers.
With its new mouth it says,
In my most considered opinion . . .
In its belly heart it says, I like sweet things.
The belly attends the meetings of university professors.
With its new lips it says,
When one considers what is reasonable and just . . .
Deep inside it says, I like soft things.
The belly talks to a beautiful woman.
With its new teeth it says,
There is much truth in your argument . . .
In its belly heart it says, I want your cunt.
The belly travels and travels.
Wherever it goes people are impressed.
How smart it is, how terribly kind.
When the belly was a belly, it was always hungry.
Now that it's a brain it has gotten very fat.
What are the loves of the belly?
Anything vulnerable and unprotected,
anything desired by anyone else.
What are the fears of the belly?
Sharp things, things with teeth, bigger bellies.
What are the dreams of the belly?
Floating through space the belly comes to the edge
of the universe and sees the alternative universe

floating toward it. In fact, it sees itself
floating toward it. The belly and alternative belly
both open their mouths very wide.
Starlight flickers across their steel teeth.
Their lips touch like the lips of lovers.
Then they disappear—plus one
and minus one cancelling themselves out.
No drum rolls or flashes of light, no screams.
Such is the joy of self gorging on self,
leaving in its wake only the smallest of sounds,
a single wrinkle in the smooth fabric of the night,
something like a hiccup, something like a sob.

DESIRE

A woman in my class wrote that she is sick
of men wanting her body and when she reads
her poem out loud the other women all nod
and even some of the men lower their eyes

and look abashed as if ready to unscrew
their cocks and pound down their own dumb heads
with these innocent sausages of flesh, and none
would think of confessing his hunger

or admit how desire can ring like a constant
low note in the brain or grant how the sight
of a beautiful woman can make him groan
on those first spring days when the parkas

have been packed away and the bodies are staring
at the bodies and the eyes stare at the ground;
and there was a man I knew who even at ninety
swore that his desire had never diminished.

Is this simply the wish to procreate, the world
telling the cock to eat faster, while the cock
yearns for that moment when it forgets its loneliness
and the world flares up in an explosion of light?

Why have men been taught to feel ashamed
of their desire, as if each were a criminal
out on parole, a desperado with a long record
of muggings, rapes, such conduct as excludes

each one from all but the worst company,
and never to be trusted, no never to be trusted?
Why must men pretend to be indifferent as if each
were a happy eunuch engaged in spiritual thoughts?

But it's the glances that I like, the quick ones,
the unguarded ones, like a hand snatching a pie
from a window ledge and the feet pounding away;
eyes fastening on a leg, a breast, the curve

of a buttock, as the pulse takes an extra thunk
and the cock, that toothless worm, stirs in its sleep,
and fat possibility swaggers into the world
like a big spender entering a bar. And sometimes

the woman glances back. Oh, to disappear
in a tangle of fabric and flesh as the cock
sniffs out its little cave, and the body hungers
for closure, for the completion of the circle,

as if each of us were born only half a body
and we spend our lives searching for the rest.
What good does it do to deny desire, to chain
the cock to the leg and scrawl a black X

across its bald head, to hold out a hand
for each passing woman to slap? Better
to be bad and unrepentant, better to celebrate
each difference, not to be cruel or gluttonous

or overbearing, but full of hope and self-forgiving.
The flesh yearns to converse with other flesh.
Each pore loves to linger over its particular story.
Let these seconds not be full of self-recrimination

and apology. What is desire but the wish for some
relief from the self, the prisoner let out
into a small square of sunlight with a single
red flower and a bird crossing the sky, to lean back

against the bricks with the legs outstretched,
to feel the sun warming the brow, before returning
to one's mortal cage, steel doors slamming
in the cell block, steel bolts sliding shut?

How difficult it was to look at them
and how hard it has been to come to the memory—
a room full of elderly nuns on the top floor
of a hospital in Kalamazoo more than twenty years ago.
I was still in graduate school and taking a break
to earn money and write, and I recall
writing a poem about Ulysses coming back
and another about a quest. How simple it seemed
to pick a life and have that life make sense.
That was what was easy about being twenty-four.
So it felt correct to choose what seemed hardest,
where the spiritual return was greatest.
That year I worked at a Catholic college
and my closest friend was a nun of about eighty
plagued by bad feet, which was why she'd been sent
to the hospital. At that time the nuns still wore
the full habit, black of course, with only
their hands and face uncovered and a great
silver cross around their necks. One never saw
their hair or any trace of their bodies, everything
was concealed in the service of their calling,
and I was struck by their wedding rings—these brides
of Christ. Clearly, I was nervous about visiting
my friend, of seeing a whole floor of sick nuns,
afraid of seeing one undressed or somehow revealed,
so it was at least a week before I finally went.
I was also writing a novel and had constant plans,
a whole career under way, and the next year back
in graduate school I even wrote a poem about this visit,
although I didn't get it right or really know
what it meant, had only been amazed, even shocked,
when I had walked down the hall, and then stopped
to look through the doorway of a ward—twenty or
twenty-five women in their eighties and nineties

propped up in chairs and couches, their habits askew,
their wimples twisted to reveal a hank of hair,
stick figures lost within yards of black cloth.
But more striking than the nuns were the dolls
that at least a dozen held—rocking and soothing them,
patting their backs, clucking and cooing to them.
One singing in a cracked voice, another clutching
the doll to her bony shoulder. How much love they had
for these rag things as they stroked and caressed them
and I remember one nun by the door with her face
scrunched into a thousand wrinkles as she aped
the doting expression of a young mother. And then
came my shock at the dolls themselves:
colorless and faceless, with their features
rubbed off, stroked, kissed off, until from
top to bottom they had turned uniformly gray,
some yarn for the hair, nothing for the eyes,
handed on from one elderly nun to another,
a comfort in their last years, before death plucked
those childless women from their chosen calling.

He must have been born with greased feet
to keep sliding so, born at the pinnacle
of a glass hill and then released,

a life spent in the articulation
of hellos and good-byes. How many times
has he carried boxes through doorways?

The key turns in the ignition, the view
in the rearview mirror repeats itself
and once more his tires caress the road,

their only love. He had hoped to stop this.
He had thought that by buying things
he could hang possessions from his body

like sandbags from a balloon. He had thought
that by acquiring a wife and family
he was at last planting himself, his two feet

sunk knee-deep in concrete, but anything
can be packed and his children's heads
peek cunningly from their cartons.

At best he can slow the rate of departure,
not move faster and faster, to take pleasure
in the experienced moment, not the next one,

the potential one. Still, he has often seen,
when returning to visit some place he had
left some years before, the same people

sitting at the same tables in the same cafés,
the same jokes, same love affairs, the same
houses being painted over and over, lives

．．．

fixed like stones along a stream, watching
the water chortle by, the same weather,
even the same birds twittering overhead.

Better fashion from his life a boat
with nothing to catch him but time itself,
that distant cataract. Better take with him

only those few possessions he values—
the wing of a sparrow to remind him
of his loyalties, a blue glass marble

to teach him the folly of standing still
and a box of air, pure air, to show him
where he has come from and what lies ahead.

Shy defiers of the existential world,
you draw your veil across the unpleasant,
then the head turns away, the body turns away,
the feet trudge off toward someplace nice, but you,
you were the first, you drew the initial curtain.

Oh, cautious celebrators of the decorous,
how much has gone unwitnessed or unjudged,
how much remains unchanged due to your benign
interference? Why reduce the world to this
middle range of behavior, as if the story

contained only happy couples on lawn chairs
nibbling macaroons and sipping soothing drinks.
Don't you fear the darkness will squeeze you tight
because of your ignorance of it?
Oh, my shy ones, forgive this desecration—

the chrome of the scissors will sparkle in your eyes,
while your being closed only simplifies my task.
A few quick snips and the light will shine forever.
Gaze upon it. See that fire, those cold stones.
This is the world to love. There is no other.

THE BODY'S CURSE

Sad to say there's more than one—loneliness
for example. What a devil. No one understands you,
no one wants to touch you, while the skin grows cold
and the mind has all the vigor of wet paper.

Yet I know people who are so distrustful
of the folks around them that when anyone gets
too close, they push them away. Get lost, they say.
Of course they are miserable, the poor babies,

but they think it is better to be tough from the start,
than to have some trickster turn on them later.
Loneliness for them is what's safest, although
no one is happy or likes getting up in the morning,

no one sings in the shower. And then there's pride:
that sense of self that says the self's first rate.
But how hungry it gets, how malnourished, yet how
it poisons the world. I knew a fellow who received

a great gift and because someone he despised
was given an equal gift he destroyed his own.
His pride made each thing smaller than it was,
leaving him bitter, dissatisfied. And then

we have opinions, those conclusions which say
that what you don't know doesn't count: the ballot box
is closed, the votes are tallied and the decision
is reached that the world is flat or she loves you

not or that man's a fool. So even the smartest
grow ignorant and stumble through the twilight
like all the rest. And then ambition, that quest
to leave the road behind one packed with monuments

to one's own perfection, a statue in the park
to show the world one isn't the jerk one thinks
in those dark moments of the night. Or sexual hunger,
thirsting for ladies as a bowling ball thirsts for pins,

then casting them aside, the beauty forgotten
while still clasped in a post-orgasmic embrace.
Greed, gluttony, sloth—but don't they all
go back to loneliness, that sense of a barrier

between oneself and others, as if they see differently,
feel differently, as if one were a dog surrounded
by skeptical cats? And so a man develops pride,
ambition and all the rest, just to prove

that the awful place with which he has been blessed
is a blessing after all. He may seem miserable—
the loneliness gnawing him like a cancer—
but actually that pain is the pain of success,

and he makes his little smile that creaks
and walks on, while what he really wants
is to be held and stroked and be told: Poor thing.
Yet even were he to get it he would break it,

like someone giving him a ceramic plate,
he would hurl it to the sidewalk, hitch up
his pants and hobble away. What can be done?
Who can say what another man wants?

Ask the mouth, it says More. Ask the feet,
they say Faster. Try the hands, they say Mine.
Question the whole crazy and quarrelsome
conglomeration, and it says Touch me.

CÉZANNE AND ZOLA

At thirteen they were known as the inseparables.
"Opposites by nature," wrote Zola, "we became
united forever in the midst of the brutal gang
of dreadful dunces who beat us." Inconsolable
with Zola in Paris, Cézanne wrote, "I no longer
recognize myself. I am heavy, stupid and slow."
Despite many visits, their disagreements overthrew
their intimacy and they grew apart. "A dreamer,"
was how Zola described his friend, "a failure
of genius." And in a novel he wrote how Cézanne
"had lost his footing and drowned in the dazzling
folly of art." Cézanne replied with sixteen years
of silence, yet when Zola died he fled to his room.
"All day," a friend said, "we heard the sound of weeping."

"Like a child," Mary Cassatt said, describing
how Cézanne resembled a cutthroat, but seemed gentle,
and that he ate scraping his soup plate, pouring
the last drops into his spoon, was deferential
to the stupid maid, held his chop in one hand,
ripping the meat with his teeth, clutched his knife
in his clenched fist the entire meal, a kind
of baton to accompany each word, each loud laugh.
"Appearances cannot be relied on over here,"
she wrote, impressed, but thinking him outrageous.
"Isolation is all I'm good for," he said in a letter,
"then at least no one gets me in his clutches."
While another painter quoted him to prove him mad:
"I am the only one alive who can paint a red."

LONG STORY

There must have been a moment after the expulsion
from the Garden when the animals were considering
what to do next and just who was in charge.
The bear flexed his muscles, the tiger flashed
his claws, and even the porcupine thought himself
fit to rule and showed off the knife points
of his quills. No one noticed the hairless creatures,
with neither sharp teeth, nor talons, they were too puny.
It was then Cain turned and slew his own brother
and Abel's white body lay sprawled in the black dirt
as if it had already lain cast down forever.
What followed was an instant of prophetic thought
as the trees resettled themselves, the grass
dug itself deeper into the ground and all
grew impressed by the hugeness of Cain's desire.
He must really want to be boss, said the cat.
This was the moment when the animals surrendered
the power of speech as they crept home to the bosoms
of their families, the prickly ones, the smelly ones,
the ones they hoped would never do them harm.
Who could envy Cain his hunger? Better to be circumspect
and silent. Better not to want the world too much.
Left alone with the body of his brother, Cain began
to assemble the words about what Abel had done
and what he had been forced to do in return.
It was a long story. It took his entire life
to tell it. And even then it wasn't finished.
How great language had to become to encompass
its deft evasions and sly contradictions,
its preenings and self-satisfied gloatings.
Each generation makes a contribution, hoping
to have got it right at last. The sun rises
and sets. The leaves flutter like a million
frightened hands. Confidently, we step forward
and tack a few meager phrases onto the end.

Once, taking a train into Chicago
from the west, I saw a message
scrawled on a wall in the railway yard—
Tommy, call home, we need you—
and for years I have worried, imagining
the worst scenarios. Beneath the message
was a number written in red chalk,
although at eighteen who was I to call
and at forty-six who is left to listen?
But Tommy, I think of him still traveling
out in the country, riding freight car
after freight car, just squeaking by
in pursuit of some private quest.
That's the problem, isn't it?
Coming into the world and imagining
some destination for oneself,
some place to make all the rest
all right, as we cast aside those
who love us, as they cast aside others
in their turn, and all of us
wandering, wandering in a direction
which only our vanity claims to be forward,
while the messages fall away like pathetic cries—
come back, call home, we need you.

NO MAP

How close the clouds press this October first
and the rain—a gray scarf across the sky.
In separate hospitals my father and a dear friend
lie waiting for their respective operations,
hours on a table as surgeons crack their chests.
They were so brave when I talked to them last
as they spoke of the good times we would share
in the future. To neither did I say how much
I loved them, nor express the extent of my fear.
Their bodies are delicate glass boxes
at which the world begins to fling its stones.
Is this the day their long cry will be released?
How can I live in this place without them?
But today is also my son's birthday.
He is eight and beginning his difficult march.
To him the sky is welcoming, the road straight.
Far from my house he will open his presents—
a book, a Swiss Army knife, some music. Where
is his manual of instructions? Where is his map
showing the dark places and how to escape them?

HOW COULD YOU EVER BE FINE

I dreamt last night I heard someone speak your name,
two women were talking about you and I went to them
and asked about you and they gave me your number.
So I called you and we talked and you said
you were fine, and I doubted it was really you,
because how could you ever be fine? What have
twenty years done to you? Where are you now?
You had the smoothest skin, a face like a beautiful
wax figure as you moved from one messed-up man
to another. There was one who used to shoot up
Jack Daniel's, and when I told him that was stupid,
he said, That's right, I'm stupid, I'm really stupid,
somebody should kill me! Until I said it actually
wasn't so stupid just to calm him. But all those men
who hit you and abused you and how you explained
they must have been right or else they wouldn't
have done it. I was too tame, didn't stick myself
with pins or know the names for all the drugs,
and had a vague idea of what I wanted to do
next week, next year. You would listen with one
black eye swollen half shut, then go back to the guy
who had done it so he could blacken the other.
I remember you told me how your mother had said
it was your duty to love her, and you shouted, No,
and kept shouting no. And when she died you felt glad,
but years later I took you to one funeral director
after another so you could find her ashes.
You said you wanted to talk to her, a beautiful
woman telling her troubles to a cardboard box.
Then you would sprinkle her ashes into the canal
and feel something, you weren't sure what, maybe
just done with something, the sense that something
was over. But either we couldn't find the right
funeral director or the ashes were already gone,

and that night you went back to a man who beat you,
and shortly after that you slipped out of my life—
a few cards, a few phone calls, then nothing.
Right now you are either out there or you're not—
smoking a cigarette, touching a sore place, looking
from the window and letting all the old faces
drift across your mind. It is hard to think of you
dowdy and forty, the problems dealt with, a life
of some sort on track, hard to think of you making it
past twenty-five. At least in books we know the end,
know the characters died or got married, had great
success or failure. But you are out there someplace,
and your friend who shot up the Jack Daniel's,
and the guy I took the knife away from,
and the other who wanted to be a writer,
and the girl who quit school to have a baby,
and another girl who smashed the doors of my truck
on an acid trip. They are all out there, just
putting one foot in front of another, just like
the torturers are out there, and the men who worked
on firing squads, and the men who like to hit things
just to hurt them. And you are out there too,
picking your way between the paper, the tin cans,
the broken glass. You had the most wonderful smile.
On whom does it shine now, who does it welcome?
People on hard streets dragged to inevitable ends.

for S.C.

NOSES

Little emissary to tomorrow,
the nose precedes us into the future,
reaching the next moment a moment before us,
a delicate Columbus of uncharted seas.
How brave is its unguarded fragility:
quick to sniffle, easily broken,
ever ready with its shout of warning,
the sneeze. True, the foot may get there
first, but it is cushioned by the shoe
and so for it the world remains abstract.
But the nose—tiny rosebud of the mole,
galumphing snout of the moose, bump
of the skunk, smidgin of the frog—
easier to imagine a heaven full of noses
than one full of people, clouds packed
with those soft triangles of flesh.

So this morning I watch my wife's nose
as she sleeps, my fingers hovering
inches above it only to stroke it.
If it were just a matter of noses,
her nose and mine,
how could we ever quarrel or fight?
No harsh words or angry looks.
How could there be anything but love
between these sweet upside down heart shapes?

SPLEEN

Oh, much maligned one, meager hunkerer
beneath the heart, they slander you
who claim that anger is your little engine,
that melancholy squats within you
like a frog in its dank grotto. My hands
feel anger, my fingers feel anger, but you
in your basement chamber, you doze to the steady
whoosh of my lungs, diminutive car wash
of the blood, extracting a few dead cells
like a monkey picking lice from its mate,
but nothing serious, nothing professional
like the liver—for you it is simply a hobby.
I knew a doctor once who had a bookcase full
of your brothers and sisters preserved in bottles
while their former hosts still strolled the streets.
I asked, Do those people persist
in feeling anger? Do they ever grow sad?
He thought I was crazy and drove me away.
But a friend with a missing spleen still
fights and rages in shoddy bars or stares out
at the moon racing behind clouds and weeps.

Little tousler of tired erythrocytes,
do they mean to say that without you
my love of life would flow unchecked,
a constant good humor untainted
by proof of falsehood, injustice or greed?
If true, then bankers would have made sure
centuries ago that each child's spleen
would be plucked out at birth, and the courts
would have declared you a common criminal,
known for your tangle of mood changes
concerning unlimited buying and spending.
No, my pygmy pacifist, my anger is my own.

It is the sweetener I use to taste the world.
It trickles from my body like sweat.
How could my love be so great if that love
throbbed unqualified? Return to sleep,
oh superfluous one, and we'll stand sentry
above your uselessness—I with my doubting,
my anger with its club, and melancholy
with its constant image of a double world:
the one, our burden, and the other, our dream.

THE BODY'S HOPE

Whatever lifts the body up—muscles,
sinews, joints; whatever wrestles against
gravity itself—the raised step, the lifted arm—
these form the body's hope. But also hunger,

selfishness, desire, all that leads us
to put one foot in front of the other,
these too form the body's hope, whatever
combats that urge to lie down—greed,

anger, lust—these feelings keep us going,
while the imagination sketches pictures
of the desired future, how we will look
in that new hat, how we will feel

with a belly full of cherries: anything
that shoves us from this moment to the next,
motivation like a flight of stairs, and hope
like a push at the top, not dissatisfaction

but eagerness to plunge into the next second:
hope like a policeman urging the crowd along,
the travel agent with enticing descriptions
of where to go next, the tour guide director

with someplace specific to get to before dark.
You know those French chateaux where you stop
for a few hours on a summer afternoon,
how you are ushered through the ornate front doors,

shown the bed where Louis the Something slept,
the chairs where Madame de Maintenon sat,
then you are shown through a door in the back,
and it is over and the peacocks cry their

abrasive cries and you return to your cars?
Life struggles to copy that French chateau,
while hope is the person leading you through
with promises of the splendor of the next room.

But the great bed looks fusty and hard,
and the chair is just a chair and on the way out
you pass tourists coming in and you want to tell them
not to bother, but hope has you by the arm.

Without hope we'd still be learning how to crawl,
while thinking, What's the point? We'd still
be staring into our first bowl of porridge
and fiddling with our spoons. Hope moves our feet.

It is the constant encourager, the enemy
of the stationary, the promiser of better moments.
In the next room waits a woman to curl our toes,
then a twelve-pound diamond, then the prize

to raise us higher than all the rest—oh, why
aren't we running faster?—hope: our dearest
enemy, slick-talking advance man for death itself,
and the back door beckons and the peacocks cry.

He hungered for the fame of Bouguereau,
his country's best-loved painter, but distrusted
how such ambition touched his art, and so
to toughen himself with irony and feel disgusted
with his wish for public acclamation he bought
a parrot and taught it to repeat as he worked: Cézanne
is a great painter, which joke gave him the doubt
to paint for the painting itself. But critical scorn
and public mockery hurt him and around that time
he painted *The House of the Hanged Man* with its tangle
of sharp angles, winter trees, thick walls of stone,
the labyrinthine flecks of green, the triangles
like knives around a wedge of country, and a scrap
of blue sky stretching above it—oh, blessèd escape.

He was a hard painter to pose for. Hours stuck
in the same spot, while he grumbled and fussed,
up to a hundred sittings till his nerves broke
and he junked the canvas and heaped abuse
on the unlucky model, friend or wife,
who had sat for weeks for absolutely no point.
His still lives took so long the flowers died,
forcing him to use paper flowers, wax fruit.
And so he would often paint himself. Only he
had the persistence to outlast his gaze,
but in each case something lies behind the calm,
perhaps a question or trace of uncertainty,
not of some weakness of his eye, but surprise
at the grim and outcast creature he had become.

The Nazi within me thinks it's time to take charge.
The world's a mess; people are crazy.
The Nazi within me wants windows shut tight,
new locks put on the doors. There's too much
fresh air, too much coming and going.
The Nazi within me wants more respect. He wants
the only TV camera, the only bank account,
the only really pretty girl. The Nazi within me
wants to be boss of traffic and traffic lights.
People drive too fast; they take up too much space.
The Nazi within me thinks people are getting away
with murder. He wants to be boss of murder.
He wants to be boss of bananas, boss of white bread.
The Nazi within me wants uniforms for everyone.
He wants them to wash their hands, sit up straight,
pay strict attention. He wants to make certain
they say yes when he says yes, no when he says no.
He imagines everybody sitting in straight chairs,
people all over the world sitting in straight chairs.
Are you ready? he asks them. They say they are ready.
Are you ready to be happy? he asks them. They say
they are ready to be happy. The Nazi within me wants
everyone to be happy but not too happy and definitely
not noisy. No singing, no dancing, no carrying on.

IN A ROW

The mailman handing me a letter,
he paid a little. My daughter's

third grade teacher, the electrician
putting a light over my back door:

they paid as well. The woman at the bank
who cashes my check. She paid a part of it.

The typist in my office, the janitor
sweeping the floor—they paid some too.

The movie star paid for it. The nurse,
the nun, the saint, they all paid for it—

a photograph from Central America,
six children lying neatly in a row.

One day I was teaching or I sold
a book review or I gave a lecture

and some of the money came to me
and some rolled off into the world,

but it was still my money, the result
of my labor, each coin still had my name

printed across it, and I went on living,
passing my days in a box with a tight lid.

But elsewhere, skulking through tall grass,
a dozen men approached a village. It was hot;

the men made no noise. See that one's cap,
see the button on that other man's shirt,

. . .

hear the click of the cartridge as it slides
into its chamber, see the handkerchief

which that man uses to wipe his brow—
I paid for that one, that one belongs to me.

SHAVING

It is really the most minuscule thing,
but you see sometimes when I shave,
my daughter follows me into the bathroom
to watch—she's sixteen months—and each
time she insists that I take the brush,
smear it around the lather in the cup,
then dab a small lump onto her hand,
which she studies, intently. Some mornings
I must do this five or six times before
I'm done scraping the remnants of yesterday
from my face. The brush is from a past life,
the present of an ex-girlfriend, and it's
at least ten times my daughter's age.
As for the badger, whose bristles
we are sharing, it must have been Swiss,
like the brush, and long turned to dust.
But I watch my daughter in the glass
and her pleasure seems so simple that I
don't mind the bother as she pokes
the lather, sniffs it, tastes it and
smears it over her hands and face up there
on the third floor of the house where I
shave in a small bathroom without windows.
I am forty-five. I had never thought,
actually, that to have a child at my age
would be different than any other age.
Probably, I'm even more patient. But
I think how in twenty years when she
is getting started, I'll be checking out,
that is, if all goes right between times.
Let them keep it, I've always thought.
Let them fend off the impending collapse.
But you know those parties where late at night
the whole place starts busting apart—

too many arguments, too many fights,
and you're just as glad to get moving,
that's how I always thought I would feel,
stepping into the big zero, but now
I see I'll be abandoning my daughter
there in the midst of the recklessness:
the bully with grabby hands, the lout
eager to punch somebody out, and my daughter,
who, in these musings while I shave,
is still under three feet tall and poking
at the lather smeared across her hand.
I joke, you know, I say we're raising her
to be the girlfriend of a Russian soldier,
or next week she'll begin karate lessons
and learn to smash carrots with a single blow.
But it all comes back as I watch her
in the mirror. Who is going to protect her?
Even now anything could happen. Last summer,
for instance, I rented a cottage from a fellow
who had a place up the hill, and one day I heard
these bees whipping past me, and you know what?
It was him, my landlord fooling with his .22,
shooting beer cans off a wall with me strolling around
down below. But that's how it is all the time,
the load of bricks crashing behind us
as the flowerpot smashes at our feet.
And cancer and car accidents, everyone's
got stories. How can I not think of this
when I watch my daughter messing
with the shaving lather? The whole
world gets vague and insubstantial, like
putting your finger through a wet tissue,
the muggers, rapists, terrorists, the bomb.
It's just luck whether you escape or get hit,

making you feel about as safe as a lightbulb
in a hailstorm which, of course, is exactly
how it is, except worse. But to have a child
means to expand the dimensions of the dark place,
until I wind up imagining this small
blindfolded creature toddling out on a rope
over the abyss and it's my daughter, my daughter,
this sweet morsel left over at the violent party,
this Russian girlfriend of the future. Well,
some mornings such thoughts crowd in on me
when I go upstairs to shave, and she
comes toddling after. That lather is so soft,
such a fragile conglomeration of white bubbles,
such a minuscule smidgin of possibility,
maybe that's why she likes it, dabbing it
with one finger, lifting it up, right there
by the pink ceramic toilet and torn green
shower curtain with silhouettes of fish,
sniffing this small heap of white bubbles,
touching it to her nose, then puff, just
blowing gently, so the bubbles hang, floating,
floating, and then they're gone of course.

In early autumn, there's a concerto
possible when there's a guest in the house
and the guest is taking a shower and the host
is washing up from the night before.
With each turn of the tap in the kitchen,
the water temperature increases or drops
upstairs and the guest responds with little groans—
cold water for low notes, hot water for high.
His hair is soapy, the tub slippery
and with his groaning he becomes the concerto's
primary instrument. Then let's say the night
was particularly frosty and now the radiators
are knocking, filling the house with warmth,
and the children are rushing around outside
in the leaves before breakfast, calling after
their Irish setter whose name is Cleveland.
And still asleep, the host's wife is making
those little sighs one makes before waking,
as she turns and resettles and the bed creaks.
Standing at the sink, the host hums to himself
as he thinks of the eggs he'll soon fry up,
while already there's the crackle of bacon
from the stove and a smell of coffee. The mild groans
of the guest, the radiator's percussion,
children's high voices, the barking of a dog,
even the wife's small sighs and resettlings
combine into this autumn concerto of which
not one of the musicians is aware as they drift
toward breakfast and then a leisurely walk
through the fields near the house—two friends
who haven't seen each other for over a year.
Much later they will remember only a color,
a golden yellow, and the sound of their feet
scuffling the leaves. A day without rancor

or angry words, the sort of day that builds a life,
becoming a soft place to look back on,
and geese, geese flying south out of winter.

for Ken Rosen

INAPPROPRIATE GESTURES

A butcher glances through a bank window and sees
a holdup in progress. Grabbing his backpack,
he thrusts bratwurst at the first ten people he meets.

A baker is witness to a dreadful murder. Two thugs
kill a nun with a folding chair. The baker dials
the zoo and asks how long the zebra has been sick.

A candlestick maker comes home to find her hubby
in bed with a floozy. Horrified, she snatches up
their Irish setter and hurls it into the Jacuzzi.

We are surrounded by inappropriate gestures.
The house is on fire. Quick, grab a tomato!
Bobby fell in the well. Hurry, play the trombone!

Let's say there was a plague or terrible war.
Everywhere people would be pulling on galoshes,
dancing the two-step, buying rabbits like crazy.

These gestures keep the future at a distance,
like a painted backdrop of cows and green fields
to hang between us and the fixed course of events.

But time is like a fat man at a banquet table—
he gobbles up the future and shits it into the past.
If we listen, we can even hear him chewing: days come,

days gone, days come, days gone. Who will save us?
We are lackluster virgins which the mustachioed world
ties to the train tracks of tomorrow's locomotive.

SWEAT

Lacrimae of the body, for whom do you weep?
What are your griefs, fears? Do you have a favorite
someplace whom violent motion makes you remember?
Does exertion bring her figure to mind and you sob?

Or is it for stasis that you mourn, complete
inaction, no past, no future, all muscles at rest.
Or are these drops not tears but the celebration
of the body's flavor: as a roast in the oven

will exude droplets of juice, so the body
in exertion is always cooking? Or perhaps
you are liquid refreshment, the body's nectar,
so that I should run and jump, then scrape myself

with a wine glass, and drink a toast. Here's
to myself—sweet days, sweet nights and the salt
taste of sweat. But no, these drops are tears.
Exertion or heat make the body recollect

what it strives to forget, eventual immobility,
the grave's invitation, as if the body
in motion were bedeviled by contrast—action
reminding it of inaction, time of time's

completion, which leads the body to remember
those days when, pink and smelling of talcum,
its movements were the focus of all attention,
and its parents bent over it with moony smiles

and gentle pats, leading it once again to thoughts
of extinction, as if the body were truly baking,
and death the moment when it is taken from the oven.
For whom does the body in motion weep? It weeps

for itself and the tears roll from its forehead
and the shirt sticks to its back, and dark circles,
like circles under the eyes after a sleepless night,
dark circles stain its clothes beneath the armpits.

THE BODY'S STRENGTH

The mind may not mind death. It means
at last letting go, the inevitable
capitulation. After all, it's tired,
very tired. But the body fights
right to the end. Up, it keeps saying,
you must get up. Think how the body combines
the most improbable collection of parts
from toenail to earlobe, kneecap
to armpit, all with different
functions and desires like a room packed
with the strangest people possible—
rabbit punchers to perfume sippers,
hot-dog maniacs to telepathic Chinese,
yet even the smallest pore keeps saying,
Keep moving. One might think the aging body
is like the donkey, while the mind
is like the man with the whip perched
on the overladen cart, but really it's
the opposite with the donkey plodding
dumbly ahead and the man shouting stop.
What keeps it going? What does the body
enjoy? At the end it can hardly hear much,
taste much, see much, smell much and a lot
just hurts, but still the body must delight
in the feel of itself even when it says ouch,
must love the touch of flesh against bones,
like a young girl wearing a silk dress
for the first time. And then it's stubborn,
one foot plopped down after another—
that's how those pyramids got built.
Get a cut, skin closes up; eat some poison,
stomach pukes it out; suffer heartbreak,
the eyes locate a new cutie pretty quick;
get sick and the white cells gang up

to kick the intruder out. Don't stop,
don't stop—the heart a valentine metronome,
a drill sergeant calling out cadence,
the clock hurrying us on to the next second,
but also, luckily, the switch which at last
clicks off, otherwise we would be like turtles
flipped over in the dirt with four feet
pumping the air, pumping the air
and no place left to get to.

Nearly friendless, with only a few years to live,
Cézanne committed to memory Baudelaire's poem
"The Carrion" in which the speaker reminds his love
of a corpse they had seen on the road, a woman
with her legs raised in the air like a tart's,
swollen with gas, crawling with maggots and flies,
a dog crouched nearby ready to resume its feast,
and the poet remarks: this will be you when you die.
Cézanne recited this poem as he painted,
finishing his still lives of skulls on a table.
He liked how Baudelaire claimed to have rescued
his lover's essence while the rats squabbled
over her corpse. The poem kept things clear:
like what slips by and what one keeps painting for.

CÉZANNE AND THE LOVE OF COLOR

Because his wife refused to miss a dress fitting,
she missed his death instead. He painted to the last,
a portrait in profile of his gardener sitting
in a green light, with a sprawling shadow cast
on the wall behind him. His son too arrived too late,
preferring with his mother the rich life of Paris.
Then, thinking his fame wouldn't last and heavy in debt,
they quickly sold his paintings, foolishly reckless
in their acceptance of small sums. "You see," his wife
told Matisse, "Cézanne couldn't paint. He didn't have
the talent to complete his pictures." Her fear
cost her a fortune. At the very end of his life
Cézanne wrote, "Long live those who have the love
of color—true representatives of light and air."

It is the shoes that show the breaking point,
the complete collapse in their lives, the moment
when something just whacked them and after that

all became different. You have seen these shoes
singly or in pairs, isolated in intersections,
nestling by curbs on suburban streets, bordering

expressways or by the edge of a dirt road
in Montana or Maine, maybe on a sidewalk, even
hanging from overhead wires, a pair of sneakers

suspended from blue sky like a bird transfixed
smack in the air, sometimes a shiny black brogan,
sometimes a gym shoe missing its laces. Innocuous,

innocent, the only evidence that something
peculiar has happened. And you think of a person
who has stared at the newspaper for too long,

or has gotten too wrapped up with the news on TV,
or has spent too long listening to people
complaining about It, it being the world

and all its depredations: killings here,
famines there, the usual violent mumbo jumbo,
except these people have gotten stuck in that

cul de sac where they can't push it back
like the rest of us, can't buy a new sweater
or dress and say, Boy, I sure needed that,

and let the world slide off a little, give them
some room to swing their arms before the pictures
crowd in again: the face of someone screaming,

. . .

the ever-increasing numbers of the dead
nudging ever closer, until there occurs
an explosion inside them, some kind of attack,

and all you know is this shoe in the roadway,
this smidgin of evidence that something for somebody
went wrong. How lucky that it hasn't happened

to you yet, that the world remains distant
and abstract, hasn't overwhelmed you yet,
that your shoes are still accounted for.

But for them something snapped. Then they were
picked up, patched back together and packed off
to heal themselves. Perhaps these are the people

you see in the malls sitting hour after hour,
watching the crowds file past, the endless
buying and selling. Someone drops them off

in the morning and picks them up at night.
Sometimes they sip tea from Styrofoam cups
or nibble a hot dog or thin slice of pizza.

Sometimes they form part of the crowd watching
the baton twirling display or karate display
or some fellow showing off a vegetable scraper.

They are eager to return to us, become
part of us again, and they sit in the mall
as a place blessedly lacking past or future:

. . .

no one dies there, the world does not intrude there.
They almost feel like people again. No one
weeps there, no one gets angry, no one

yells at them or finds fault with them or tells them
to do something quick. They sit in their new shoes
studying the crowds and trying to fix themselves,

like trying to invent a new kind of smile,
an upside down one or sideways like a scar.
And they sit very quietly because they know

if they jump or move quickly they will break apart
and the custodians in their gray coveralls
will gather around these broken fragments of glass

with a little water, a little ice like a spilled drink
and even their spirits will be yelled at, even
their tentative souls. So they just watch

and try to believe in a world like this one:
no extremes of sound or color, no extremes
of emotion, everything exactly in the middle,

and no death, no death anyplace, and no cruelty.
And sometimes it works, sometimes they truly
get better. You can wait in the parking lot

and might see a man toddling out through the exit,
his arms raised for balance, taking one step
then another, blinking into the bright light,

flinching a little at the sound of traffic.
If you shouted right now you could break him.
But who wants to do that? Isn't this when

. . .

you should hurry to welcome him, to embrace him?
Wouldn't he do the same for you if your positions
were reversed and you were the one creeping back

into the world? And they are glad to be back
if only for a short time, glad for the chance
to chuckle with their families and glance around

with wonder, to reenter their passionate stories
before the world again rears up and entangles them
with the statistics of its victims, enfolds them

with all the faces of the lost, before the world
wraps its string around them and sets them spinning
between one curb and the other, while behind them

as souvenirs of the world's attention—
a black running shoe, a torn cowboy boot,
a new black pump with the heel snapped off.

HOW IT WAS AT THE END

The box was set in a hole in the ground,
a white cardboard box big enough
for a corsage, in a hole big enough for a rosebush.
It was raining; a few prayers were said.
And his granddaughter said, How did they make him so little
to put him in such a little box?
And her cousin said, How do you mean, they burned him?
A few people sprinkled dirt over the box,
but an hour later it still stood uncovered,
growing sodden as the hole filled with water.
My wife showed it to me, then went to look for a shovel.
But there was no shovel, no trowel or big spoon.
We scooped up the mud with our hands
and piled it onto the white cardboard, just enough
to cover it. Then we wiped our hands on the grass—
thick, gloppy, turd-colored, mud-smelling mud—
rubbing hard. But still we found it stuck between
our fingers or under the nails, flecks of dirt
which we picked at throughout the long afternoon.
That was three days ago and the rain keeps falling.
It is October. The leaves make their bright passage
from the trees to that nothingness called eternal.

WALLS TO PUT UP, WALLS TO TAKE DOWN

The old madhouse in Santiago stood tucked back
behind the hospital on a side street to the cemetery,
walls of cheap brick, cheap concrete through which
the inmates had bored little holes, and walking past

one could see dozens of cleft sticks with notes
offered to the passersby, some begging for money,
others for help or food, some asking that word be sent
to some friend or relative or lover who surely

must be waiting just as they themselves had waited,
all day holding their sticks as if fishing over
a dry pond, the water seeped away, leaving several
tires, a cat skeleton tied to a brick, a rusted

car door. I remembered all this in a hotel bar
in Belgrade when a whore was telling me, "My name
is Dragonova but I prefer to be called Lolita."
Lolita the promise, Dragonova the reality,

a beautiful girl hoping to become a hairdresser,
but no matter how much I wanted her flesh, to cup
her breasts, nuzzle my nose in her belly, it was
her flesh that stood between us and what I wanted,

stood between us like the wall of the madhouse.
"A little pop," a friend said, "you should have
taken her upstairs for a little pop." But what
could we really do? She might charitably moan.

I might have my little flash of light, a meal
after which one still feels hungry. The thing is
that nobody ever went down that street in Santiago.
It was a side street. But it didn't matter, it was

the only street they had. Sometimes with my wife,
if we haven't been quarreling, it feels like
we are sitting together without skin, a large basket
of confused body parts. "In this mood," as Wordsworth

remarked, "successful composition generally begins."
It's as if I could reach her skin from the inside,
burrowing outward instead of poking at the surface
like a dowser looking for water. Flaubert in Egypt

had a wonderful whore, Kuchuk Hanem, who he swore
would remember him more than all the others.
"Toward the end," he wrote, "there was something
sad and loving about the way we touched."

Later he realized his self-deception. "This
particular tourist who was vouchsafed the honors
of her couch has vanished from her memory like
all the others." Also, "As for physical pleasure,

it must be slight, since the famous button, the seat
of such pleasure, is snipped off at an early age."
And he concludes, "Traveling makes one modest—
you see what a tiny spot you inhabit in the world."

And as a postscript: "I must tell you, my dear sir,
that I picked up in Beirut (I discovered them in Rhodes,
land of the dragon) seven chancres . . . Each night
and morning I bandage my poor prick." Recently,

in Santiago I went searching for this madhouse
and it was gone, torn down, and only a section
of wall remained through which the inmates
had pushed their sticks. A hot and smoggy day,

the streets crowded with buses, cabs. Think of
all those people in transit—all those of destinations
with one single destination waiting a little further
beyond. The mental patients, more like prisoners,

had been transferred. Or perhaps with modern medicine
they had been released and had no need to ask
for anything, plead or beg for anything, as they
proceeded in speedy transition from one less

than perfect place to the next. Do you remember
how Ford Madox Ford wrote that you marry a person
to finish a conversation with her? And I also
like how that summons up that somewhat outdated

legal expression for illicit fucking: criminal
conversation, or crim con as they said in the courts.
Many times my wife and I speak only to complain
and I am the bag of stones she wears around her neck,

but other times, fewer times, we are engaged in that
long conversation, the one we stay together for,
the one we always hope for, where the flesh seems
to disappear and the parts get all jumbled together

as in a cannibal's stew, even if she sits in one chair
and I sit in another. The whore in Belgrade knew
about one hundred words in English and half were
the specialty words of her profession. I bought her

a Coke. She asked why I was in Belgrade. In explanation
I showed her the book of my poems translated into
her language. She read a few, decided she wanted it,
asked for it, asked me to sign it, then carried it

off to her next customer, beautiful skimpily dressed
girl with a face of shadow and a book of poems.
Oh, Dragonova/Lolita sleep with it under your pillow
just once. Those inmates in Santiago could see nothing,

hear nothing. All they had were those holes and their
messages—help me, they put me here by mistake—
and years of waiting until the whole place was
torn down. And I asked my wife who knew the city,

Didn't you ever read the messages? And she said,
No one ever stopped. Some friends had told her what
the bits of paper said. At the end of the street
stood the huge granite gates of the cemetery, like

the gates of a municipal museum but bigger, a city
of corpses with its ghettos and rich neighborhoods,
rows of fancy houses although no one asks to borrow
a cup of sugar. The trouble with Belgrade, the promise

of Lolita and the actuality of Dragonova, her mad-
house walls and my madhouse walls rubbing crazily
together, what if I grew to like it? It makes me
remember an old Texan in Amsterdam in 1959—

for us teenagers the lovely Dutch whores charged
two dollars and seventy cents if any of us managed
to dredge up the nerve, for this Texan they charged
twenty-seven dollars and a lot of laughter. Still

he would stagger out each evening, his guts hurt,
kidneys hurt, his prick was wobbly and battered
as he kept banging himself against the hard Dutch flesh.
Sometimes around midnight I would find him in a bar

too depressed even to speak. He had children
somewhere, a divorced wife. What beauty gives us
is the hope of intimacy. Fashion and advertising,
the whole package, all promise a certain closeness,

an occasion when the walls might disappear,
one inmate rubbing his belly against another
belly of his choosing, or which has chosen him,
the long conversation, the erasure of isolation,

as if we might all be piled together like puppies
in a pet-shop window, a tangle of extremities
and no barriers anyplace, hardly any need to speak,
each thought anticipated and responded to,

no concern for the future, no regret for the past,
just this complete touching, this discourse
with all the barriers gone, and that's the joke,
right? Who put the walls up in the first place,

who made them indestructible and now we want them
gone? I told my wife, can you take me to that street?
So we drove through Santiago. Smog so dense
our eyes burned, but all we found were just fragments

of brick walls with little holes bored through them,
thick walls, nearly two feet of boring and digging,
then the waiting, occasionally jiggling the stick
to show someone was there, and we knew without speaking

they hadn't been released, weren't out on the street,
but that somewhere were new walls of red brick
or concrete, and on one side someone was trying to
scratch his way through with a pin to make a hole

big enough for a little note, a little request,
and on the other side the traffic, the honking,
air so thick with fumes it wipes out the mountains,
leaving just the city, its constant jittery motion.

TOTING IT UP

He bought one pair of boots, then another.
They were good boots. He had a four boots life.
He bought twelve cars. He had a twelve car life.

He had fifty-three hundred orgasms but hungered
for a few hundred more. He had two wives:
a two wife life, a four kids life, a twelve

grandchildren life. He drank thirty-four thousand
six hundred and sixty-six cups of coffee.
He ate a quarter of a ton of spaghetti.

He had five heart attacks: a five heart attack life.
He was in the hospital ten times. He had
a two cane life, a one pair of crutches life,

a one wheelchair life, a one final illness life,
and all his memories vanished like bubbles
from a glass of champagne. His last suit of clothes

turned to dust and his coffin turned to dust
more slowly. To his grandchildren he was a face,
to their children a name, and to their children

a vacancy, and over his grave a road was built,
and the world rolled down that road. See there
in the distance, that brightly disappearing speck.

THE DAY THE WORLD ENDS

El día del fin del mundo . . . yo grabaré mis iniciales en la corteza
de un tilo sabiendo que eso no sirve para nada.   —*Jorge Teillier*

The day on which the world ends will
of course be different in each place.
Here it is raining, there snowing.
Here the night shields the now inconsequential
designs of the thief, there the sun
caressing the back of a man on the beach
begins the burn which will never keep him
awake and tossing and cursing his foolishness.
Some people are laughing, some watch a train go by.
It is surprising how many at that precise moment
are eating an apple, brushing their teeth, looking off
at a cloud that resembles a dog's head, remembering
their childhood. And in one window a hand appears.
It is sunset and the sky full of promise.
The hand, a woman's, seems almost rich
in its pinkness and plumpness; oh,
what a wealth it contains as it catches
the ring, drags down the already forsaken shade.

It could be like one of those dreams
where you must carry water in your hands
for half a mile to put some fire out
and it all drips away through your fingers.

Is this forgetfulness, the world slipping away,
while confusion expands, eating our memories
like a lava flow demolishing a landscape,
thoughts like rabbits baked in their holes?

Here comes my best friend, old what's his name.
And where was that place where I first
made love and who was that girl, the one
I swore ever to be true to? The mind

like a blank screen after the film is over,
the body like the derelict in the front row
and no place to go. The mind like
frozen blue sky in the dead of winter,

the body like the shaven snow-covered fields.
But wasn't this our desire,
the destruction of past and future,
the ability to read the same page

of a book over and over and each time
we chuckle and feel amused—nothing back there
to depress one, nothing ahead to hide from,
the single moment caught like the single

syllable the stutterer is stuck upon,
or the record caught in a single groove
repeating a few organ notes of Bach forever?
But not forever, only until something

lifts the needle and then comes the silence,
the huge one hanging like a banner
between the light and the dark,
and across it is printed whose name?

THE BODY'S WEIGHT

A bookcase has its books, a horse supports its rider,
but the body's greatest burden is itself,
which it bears through the long day, fallen

from bed, pointed toward bed, as if the body
were the bed's creature, which the bed releases
in the morning much as a farmer turns a cow

out to pasture, summoning it back at night.
But the weight of the body—the skin settled
upon flesh and the flesh upon muscle,

and the muscle upon bone; the weight
of the stomach and hips, kidneys and lungs—
all this the body carries with it,

at first lightly, eager to get started,
then gladly, scarcely knowing it is there,
a bag of feathers, a silk scarf, but then,

like a naked man rooted before a mirror,
the body is introduced to the body,
and the body begins to instruct the body—

the legs begin to feel heavy, breasts feel heavy,
the back won't straighten, belly flops forward,
the neck stiffens, arms stiffen, shoulders stiffen,

even the fingers hate to bend, and creak
like the hinges of heavy doors, while the heart
curls up in its cage like a dying spider.

It is then that the whispering begins,
at first not even heard, rather sensed or felt,
like a vibration deep inside us, a shivering:

. . .

Put it down, something says, put it down.
We begin to sit more and lie down more,
and the sudden inexplicable pains come more often.

It is here that the weight of the body
becomes almost a comfort, like the weight
of a hand coaxing us to rest, even though

we want to keep going; and each day the hand
presses more firmly and all gets heavier,
as if an old man, even when thin and muscular,

bears four times the weight of a young one,
as if the weight of the whole were four, six,
ten times greater than the sum of its parts;

and each day our steps get more difficult,
as if the feet were being pressed into the dirt,
so that if the ground were soft, the body

would slide through its folds like a clothespin
being pushed into powder. How did I ever manage
anything so heavy? Is it true that I once rushed

through the day with the weight of the body
as trifling as a sweater tossed over my shoulder?
Put it down, says the voice, put it down.

And as the daily body is the bed's creature,
so the lifely body is the earth's creature,
which is where the weight of the body

. . .

is persistently urging us, pushing us toward
the single door through which we all must exit,
till at last we pass through it and stand released

and briefly we're embraced by a joyful lightness,
as light as smoke rising, or a phrase of music,
or butterfly wings, and then the darkness begins.

Some last words. A few external factors
influenced the writing of these poems.
Concurring Beasts was constantly domi-
nated by the Vietnam war and the do-
mestic craziness that accrued to it, such
as the 1968 Democratic convention in
Chicago. During that time, I moved
from graduate school to my first teaching
position to nearly two years as a general
assignment reporter for the *Detroit News,*
where, among other things, I wrote
about one hundred stories on the deaths
of Detroit-area soldiers. *Griffon* was a
breaking away, a discovery of metaphor
in Anglo-Saxon riddles, an attempt to
find a new language and new subject.

In January 1978, I was fortunate
enough to join the master of fine arts
program at Goddard College and began
teaching with Ellen Bryant Voigt, Louise
Glück, Lisel Mueller, Raymond Carver,
Tobias Wolff, Michael Ryan and
Heather McHugh. Shortly came Robert
Hass, Thomas Lux, Steve Orlen, Joan

Aleshire, Greg Orr, Michelle Simmons, Francine Prose and many others. In 1981, the program moved to Warren Wilson College and came under the direction of John Skoyles. My writing since 1978 has been deeply influenced by these writers. I have learned much from them. They demanded rigor and I attempted to respond. These poems would have been impossible without them.

The Balthus Poems were an attempt to write narrative poems devoid of autobiographical subject matter. Although each poem takes its title from a painting by Balthus, they were not intended to interpret the paintings or explain the intentions of the artist. As I wrote in the original note, "I tried to turn each painting into a personal metaphor to create narrative poems seemingly free from the lyrical first-person voice. This is not to dismiss their debt to Balthus, which is immeasurable, but my desire was to write poems that in no way would be dependent on a knowledge of the painting or the artist."

Lastly, since 1981, I have traveled often to Chile, spending in total over two years in Santiago, where my wife's family lives. I do not see myself as being influenced by Chilean poetry or magic realism, but the constant contrast between my country and a third-world country has given my work a political attentiveness and coloration which, for better or worse, I greatly value.

Stephen Dobyns is a professor of English at Syracuse University who also teaches in the MFA program at Warren Wilson College. He is the author of seven previous volumes of poetry and fifteen novels. His first book of poems, *Concurring Beasts*, was the Lamont Poetry Selection for 1971. *Black Dog, Red Dog* was the winner of the 1984 National Poetry Series competition. *Cemetery Nights* was chosen for the Poetry Society of America's Melville Cane Award in 1987.